KNOW YOU CAN

**NO MORE EXCUSES -
HOW TO BECOME FINANCIALLY FIT
IN 90 DAYS**

WESLEY J. FORSTER

Copyright © 2013 HSI Financial Group Inc.

All rights reserved. No part of this publication may be reproduced, stored in a retrieval system, or transmitted in any form or by any means, electronic, mechanical, photocopying, recording, scanning, or otherwise, without either the prior written permission of the publisher.

While the publisher and author have used their best efforts in preparing this book, they make no representations or warranties with respect to the accuracy or completeness of the contents of this book and specifically disclaim any implied warranties of merchantability or fitness for a particular purpose. No warranty may be created or extended by sales representatives or written sales materials.
The advice and strategies contained herein may not be suitable for your situation. You should consult with a professional where appropriate. Neither the publisher nor the author shall be liable for damages arising herefrom.

The author has changed and altered many of the facts and details contained herein with respect to clients of the author in his capacity as a financial planner as well as changing many of the events which are referred to herein.

This book is not to be interpreted or construed as an offering or solicitation with respect to any investments or insurance and this book is not intended to be furthering any trade with respect to any financial instrument for which the author is not licensed. Caution must be taken into consideration when making any investment due to volatility and risk. The best defense is a financial plan.

Care has been taken to trace the ownership of copyright material to use in this book. The author and publisher welcome any information enabling them to rectify any references or credit in subsequent editions.

HSI Financial Group Inc.
110 Quarry Park Boulevard S.E., Suite 140
Calgary, Alberta T2C 3G3

www.hsifinancial.com

ISBN: 1490565116

ISBN 13: 9781490565118

Library of Congress Control Number: 2013912503

CreateSpace Independent Publishing Platform
North Charleston, South Carolina

TESTIMONIALS

"Wes takes a common sense approach to financial planning that will help anyone who reads this book. This should be required reading for those wanting to maximize the full potential of their investment program!"

Harry S. Dent, Jr.
Founder and CEO, Author
HS Dent

"Books on financial planning are hard to read and boring – *all except this breezy, well informed read from experienced advisor, Wes Forster*. I have to admit, I love the analogy of tying piloting an airplane to reaching your financial goals. It adds a unique and memorable flare to working with your money and your advisor. Forster pulls no punches in *"Know You Can – How to change your financial life in 90 days"* but he does it in a fatherly advice sort of way. He tells you what you need to know but doesn't make you feel badly for not knowing it yet. He cuts through the fog on this important but crowded topic and provides common sense, every day advice that will help you reach your financial goals. If you want to improve your financial future but don't want the usual hard to read and follow gobbledygook, read Wes Forster's "Know You Can". There's nothing better than when you "know you can" retire well, reach your goals and sleep at night."

Jim Ruta
Financial Industry Speaker, Commentator and Writer
Managing Partner, LifeAssist Software, Boston

CONTENTS

Testimonials	iii
Contents	v
Preface	vii
Introduction	ix
One – How to Reach Your Destination with a Financial Plan	1
Two – Don't Waste Another Day	11
Three – Creating a Plan, Part I: Meeting Agenda, Critical Financial Events, Personal Financial Policy Statement, and Tax Planning	25
Four – Creating a Plan, Part II: Retirement Planning, Cash Flow Planning, and Educational Savings	39
Five – Creating a Plan, Part III: Your Family's Security (Insurance), and Estate Planning	53
Six – How to Ensure You Have a Good Plan	67
Seven – How Much to Pay a Financial Planner	83

Eight – Investing Doesn't Have to Be Complicated	99
Nine – Two Misconceptions about Investing	109
Ten – Investment Strategy	119
Eleven – Making Good Financial Decisions	131
Twelve – Insurance	141
Thirteen – Business Planning	161
Fourteen – Financial Harmony in the Home	173
Fifteen – Where Do We Go From Here?	183
Acknowledgments	191
About the Author	193

PREFACE

As a financial planner and a pilot, one of my biggest passions in life is helping people get to where they want to go. I love creating a sense of certainty for people that they'll get to their destination safely. But when it comes to finances, most people feel a *lot* of uncertainty. I love taking away the uncertainty, but since I can't meet and speak with every person in North America, I created this book to help.

Why do people need the help? Because the best way to take control of one's finances is to create a plan. But most people do not understand what a plan is. When new clients come to see me, many of them *think* they have a financial plan, when it's really just an investment plan. Others don't have any type of plan at all, or at least not a *written* plan. It's extremely rare. As a result, what I see most of the time is that people are confused about how to reach their financial goals, and they don't even know why they're confused. Many people aren't even positive what their financial goals are. So, people look back five, ten, twenty years and wonder why they're never getting ahead. They feel like they're reliving the same year over and over again. They feel disappointed and frustrated, but they're not sure how to change it or what even needs to be changed. And it's all because they don't have a plan.

The information in this book has helped thousands of people retire with confidence, knowing they can. At my company, HSI Financial Group Inc., we share with our clients how a plan will help take away their frustration and replace it with peace of mind. We show them how their plan will help them define what they want, what to do, and when to do it—how it will actually change their life—because reaching their goals and knowing you can is what brings peace of mind.

Another reason I wrote this book is that too many professionals in the financial services industry have become complacent. They are used to doing the bare minimum for their clients because they want to see as many people as possible without spending more time with them than they have to. They want to rush their clients out the door. But people need more help than that. They *deserve* more than that. For any financial planners reading this book, you will see how it is worth every extra minute of your time to create a thorough financial plan for your client.

I feel sorry for people who don't understand these things. I feel sorry for people who don't want to invest a short amount of time and effort to create a plan, because I know where that attitude will take them: nowhere.

I wrote this book because I don't want to see people go nowhere. I want to help everyone get to where they want to go. So, if there's somewhere you want to go, this book was written for you.

INTRODUCTION

Ask yourself this question: "Can I retire?"

Tens of thousands of people lie awake every night asking themselves the same question, or questions just like it:

"Can I survive if I lose half my wealth?"

"Can I pay to send my child to a good university?"

"Can I still do the same things I do now after I retire?"

"Can I afford to go on an extended vacation?"

"Can I take care of my family if I lose my job?"

"Can I start my own business?"

"Can I, can I, can I...?"

For most people, the answer to those questions is "I don't know." But when it comes to your finances, "I don't know" are three of the worst words you can possibly say because, more often than not, "I don't know" ends up meaning "I can't."

Nobody knows everything, and, of course, there are lots of things in life it's OK *not* to know. It's OK, for example, if you can't explain the theory of relativity, unless you're a physicist, because the theory of relativity doesn't have any bearing on how you live your life. It's OK if you can't say what year the Magna Carta was signed, unless you're trying to pass a test, because the answer doesn't determine what you do every day. But your finances are different. Finance extends to *every* part of your life—who you are, what you do, what you *want* to do—because all of these facets are shaped, at least in part, by your finances. So, if at any point you *don't* know the answer to the "Can I?" questions above, it's because you're out of touch with your finances. You don't know how much money you have or how much you need or what your options are.

Again, finances extend to every part of your life. They determine the direction your life is moving in. So, the words "I don't know" effectively mean you're flying blind. You're just guessing, or hoping, or praying you'll be able to land safely. But at any given moment, you could crash...because you *just don't know*.

No one would ever fly a plane blind. No one should ever go through life blind, either.

So, ask yourself one more time: "Can I...?"

If the answer is "I don't know," then this book is for you.

Now, ask yourself this: "Why don't I know?" I'll tell you: it's almost certainly because you don't have a plan. Most people don't. Retirement, marriage, death—these are all distant events in a nebulous future. Most people just go through life assuming they'll deal with them at some point. They'll "cross that bridge" when they come to it. But what most people don't realize is that without a plan, they'll be extremely ill-equipped to deal with those events when they do come.

As a financial advisor for over twenty-eight years, and as a commercial pilot, I've seen firsthand just how risky it is to go through life without a plan. To prove it, I've written this book to be somewhat different. You won't find simple pointers on budgeting in this book, or top ten lists on "how to plan for retirement." You won't find dry statistics or academic jargon, either. What you will find are stories. Almost every chapter contains one or more real-life stories—stories about people just like you, with many of the same dreams, circumstances, and problems you're likely to have. Actually, these stories could be about anybody: your neighbour, your friend, your sibling. It doesn't matter how much money you have because in the end, planning is about finding out how much you *need*. It's about knowing you can get there. Some of the stories have happy endings; some of them don't. But they all illustrate just how crucial planning can be.

Think of managing your finances like going on a road trip. You have a destination in mind, but instead of sitting down to plan out your journey, you just get in your car and start driving. Would you ever do something like that? I don't think so. How would you know if you were taking the right roads, if you were going in the right direction? How would you know if you were driving into trouble? What would you do if your car broke down, or you ran out of money, or got lost?

No, most people who go on road trips take the time to plan. They'll study the different routes and choose the best one. They'll determine how to pay for the trip or how to get the best deal. They'll inventory what they have and what they'll need. In short, they'll have a plan. It's a no-brainer.

So, if it's a no-brainer to plan for a simple road trip, shouldn't it be the same for life in general? If you have a destination, don't you want to know how to get there? Don't you want to *know you can*?

Yes, it's crucial to have a financial plan. But this book isn't just about making the case for a plan; it's also about how to actually create one. By the time we get to the end, you'll see exactly what should go into a plan, how to implement it, and how to find the right professional to help you along your way. This last one is especially important, and here's why:

In the airline industry, you'll often hear older pilots talk about having a "bag of luck" and a "bag of experience." In other words, all new pilots who enter the industry have two bags: a bag for luck and a bag for experience. When they start out, their bags of luck are full, but their bags of experience are empty. The goal for new pilots, old-timers will say, is to fill their bags of experience *before* their bags of luck run out. If they don't, well…you can imagine what happens then.

Here's how that applies to financial planning. You'd never try to fly a plane yourself if you didn't have the education or experience. When you want to fly, you *always* trust an experienced pilot to do the flying for you. It should be no different when it comes to your financial plan. The average person usually goes a long time before creating a plan. That means he or she has spent years, decades even, using up the bag of luck.

But how can people fill up their bags of experience? Most people have a job, a family, a personal life. They don't have the training to be a financial planner or the time to be trained in the first place. So, the best thing to do, instead, is to find someone who *does* have a bag of experience—a skilled, qualified financial planner to help get you to your destination—before your bag of luck runs out.

This book will show you how.

Know You Can is not for do-it-yourselfers. It's not for people who only rely on themselves and never want help from anybody. It's not for people who just want to pay off their house or manage their own investments. *Know You Can* is for those who want to take complete control of their financial life. It's for people who are tired of hoping, guessing, or praying, for people who want to *know* they're going to be successful, so they can spend time living instead of worrying.

Right before I put the final period on this book, a prospective client came in to see me. Hank Wilson just didn't know what to do. For the past several years, he had put his money into fancy investment programs run by famous financial celebrities, the kind you see giving interviews on TV. They'd tell him where to put his money, when to get in, and when to get out. That's all. He had no other goals in mind for his money, and these programs didn't ask him what his goals were. The only objective was to get as big a return as possible. When you think about it, it's not much different from sticking a quarter into a slot machine. You put your money in, cross your fingers, and hope you end up with the word JACKPOT reflected in your eyes.

Unfortunately for Hank, things didn't work out that way. By the time he came to see me, the only thing in his eyes was frustration. None of those programs helped him get ahead. In fact, they only set him back further. Usually, they started off pretty well, but by the time those celebrities told him to "get out," it was too late. Trying to time your investments is like riding an old, wooden roller coaster. It might be exhilarating, but it's bumpy, dangerous, and the dips can be disastrous. But having a plan is like a smooth, straight flight. Flights take you farther than roller coasters, and they're faster and safer, too.

So, Hank had a talk with Nada, his wife. Several years had passed since he started investing in those programs, and he was at the point in his life where all those future events, like retirement, no longer seemed quite so distant. They were no longer playing a game, trying to win as much money as possible. They had needs to meet, obligations to keep, and momentous life-changes just around the corner.

That's when Nada asked Hank the million-dollar question: "Hank, when can we retire?"

Hank could only reply, "I don't know."

Not long after, Hank came to see me. At first, he was skeptical. He didn't believe he'd ever be able to retire the way he wanted to.

I felt otherwise. "You just don't know what you need," I told him.

Still, he wasn't sure. What made my program so different from all these others? He wanted to know.

"For starters," I said, "with me, you're not getting a program. You're getting a plan."

So, we worked together—Hank, Nada, and my team. By the time we were done, I asked Hank how he felt now. "Both of us feel really, really good," he answered. "Especially Nada."

When Nada first asked him about their retirement, he didn't know the answer. Now he does. He knows exactly what he has to do and when to do it. Most importantly, he knows he *can* do it.

"What's the biggest benefit to having a financial plan?" I asked him.

"Before," he said, "I didn't even know if I *could* retire. Now I *know I can*."

The purpose of this book is to start you on the right path. Your goals may be far different from Hank's. The questions you ask yourself might be nothing like the ones you saw above. But no matter what you want, or where you want to go, this book will help you get started. By the time you reach the end, you'll be headed in the right direction. You won't have to wonder if you can reach your financial destination.

By the time you finish this book, you'll *know you can*.

ONE

HOW TO REACH YOUR DESTINATION WITH A FINANCIAL PLAN

You are on a plane, flying at a cruising altitude of thirty-five thousand feet. The only sound is the quiet thrum of the engines and the hushed voices of other passengers. A movie plays on the monitor above your head. When you look out the window, it seems as if you are drifting almost lazily through a sea of white.

Sounds serene, doesn't it? That's because the best airlines—and the planes they operate—go out of their way to make it so. But what you *don't* see is what's happening around you. In reality, the plane is not drifting through a sea of white: it's searing its way across the sky at a speed of nine hundred kilometers per hour. Huge jet engines are stationed on either side of you, sucking in air through massive fans and then mixing it with raging hot fuel in a combustion chamber. The exhaust is then pumped out through a nozzle in the rear. This exhaust is what gives a plane its mighty thrust.

Beneath your feet is a serpent's nest of wires and gears, sending signals and power from the cockpit to every other part of the plane. And in front of you? That's where the pilots sit, and if you think they got to where they are simply by learning which buttons to push, you're mistaken. The truth is, every time you fly in a plane, you're taking a ride inside a missile that can hurtle its way a mere ten kilometers beneath Outer Space.

Flying a plane is complicated. There are so many things a pilot has to learn—physics, for example. Flying a plane is not like driving a car, and, in fact, many of the instincts we display every day in our cars would get you killed in an airplane. Pilots have to be able to fly using complex instruments as well as their own eyes. When flying, they have to factor in speed, altitude, barometric pressure, weather conditions, and a stream of conversation between themselves and the control tower, which instructs them when to climb, when to descend, and at what altitude to be at all times. In fact, you may not realize it, but airplanes fly in spaces very similar to the lanes in which we drive our cars. Just as we can't swerve in and out of lanes on the highway, an airplane pilot can't leave his or her assigned "lane" at will. Sure, it may seem like the sky is a big place—much bigger than your average freeway—but the difference is that cars only travel about 120 kilometers per hour most of the time. Planes travel almost ten times that fast. You can cover a *lot* more distance in a second's time in a plane than you can in a car—so, no swerving!

It takes a lot to fly an airplane, far more than most passengers ever realize. If people knew how complex it was—how much time, training, thought, and effort it takes to get you airborne—they probably wouldn't relax so much when the seatbelt sign is turned off. In fact, pilots need both a tremendous amount of knowledge and an equal amount of skill because at any moment, they might need to make a split-second decision. They might encounter instrument failure, extreme weather, engine failure…even a flock of birds. In short, they might have to deal with the unexpected. And when you're flying that high, that fast, there isn't time to discuss things in committee. Pilots have to already know what to do. They have to have a *plan*.

Why am I telling you all this? After all, you picked up this book thinking it was going to be on investing or something, right?

The reason I'm telling you all this is that I have two passions in life: flying and financial planning. What constantly amazes me is how much the principles of one discipline translate into the other. No, not all financial planners are good pilots, or vice versa. But the same lessons apply. The fundamentals of good flying are also the fundamentals of making good financial decisions.

How do I know this? As I said before, I'm a commercial pilot. I'm also an expert financial planner with over twenty-eight years in the business. I fly a Cessna 340 cabin-class airplane and run my own financial planning practice called HSI Financial Group Inc.

So, I know a thing or two about both.

Ultimately, the single most important link between flying and financial planning is that in both cases, the person doing it has one goal in mind: reaching his or her destination. Whether that destination is physical or financial, whether it's flying to another country or just trying to reach retirement, flying and financial planning are both a matter of getting from point A to point B. Safely.

What, then, do *pilots* and *financial planners* have in common? They're both trained to get people to their destination. They're both trained in the theory, the laws, the rules, and the procedures of getting from point A to point B. They're both trained in navigation, in knowing the path, in anticipating turbulence, and in knowing how to handle it.

Above all, they both know the importance of creating a plan. Without a flight plan, pilots *might* be able to get to their destination—if they're lucky (though probably not). But sooner or later, something unforeseen will happen, at which point there can be only one outcome: they'll crash.

Similarly, without a financial plan, most people *might* be able to reach their financial goals—if they're lucky (though probably not). In fact, most people don't even have real goals until they set about creating a plan. But sooner or later, something will happen that they didn't expect. Sure, most people don't go through life at thirty-five thousand feet. But, without a plan, when the unexpected happens, there's usually one outcome: they'll crash. The wreckage of a plane and the wreckage of a person's finances might not look the same, but trust me, they're just as hard to put back together.

In life, your finances are like your own personal airplane. If you want to get anywhere in this world, it'll be your finances that get you there. And like an airplane, personal finances are *complicated*. You may not think about it day to day, but your finances are a huge, complex system, consisting of taxes, investments, income, savings, debt, your estate, insurance, expenses, cash flow, and more. That's not even mentioning all the different *kinds* of taxes there are, or forms of income, or types of investments—each with its own set of rules, pitfalls, and opportunities, many of which you are probably unaware. Every day you've got money coming in and money going out, some of it for the short term, some of it for the long term, and the decisions you make can have a *massive* impact on the balance. And, like an airplane, things can change in the blink of an eye—sometimes disastrously.

Pilots combat that risk—and the complexity of flying—by filing flight plans. Flight plans are documents that list the pilot's

- point of departure,

- point of arrival,

- estimated flight time (handy so that authorities will know if a plane is overdue),

- planned altitude (so that aircraft controllers can help keep planes separated),

- the amount of fuel on board,

- planned airspeed,

- number of passengers,

- colour of the plane,

- planned route,

- alternate routes, and

- alternate destinations (in case of emergency).

All are critical for both the pilot and for aviation authorities. For pilots, flight plans help ensure that all the details necessary to fly have been taken care of and are not overlooked; moreover, they remind pilots what contingencies to take in case of emergencies. This way, if the unexpected happens, pilots do not waste valuable time wondering what to do. Thus, flight plans lessen the chance of them making a mistake.

So, how does this relate to your finances? Why are you holding this book?

Because, again, your finances are your own personal plane. They get you where you need to go. They're complex. And if you're not careful, they can fall apart. They are simply too important in life to be casual about. Your health, your home, and even your happiness all depend on it. Don't believe me? Think of every goal you've ever had in life. Landing your dream job? Most dream jobs require an education, which you have to pay for. Owning a home? That's a big part of finance, too. Travelling the world? Wanting to retire? Achieving *any* of those things depends on the state of your finances. Even if your goals don't directly involve money, chances are that the better shape your finances are in, the easier it'll be to pursue them.

Now, think of your values. What do you care about in life? Your health? The future and well-being of your family? Your hobbies? Charity work? Those things have to be paid for.

I don't necessarily believe that this world "revolves around money" or that life should be spent solely looking to gain more. Far from it. What I *do* believe—what I *know*—is that like an airplane, money is a means to an end. It's what you need to get to your destination, to reach your goals, and to protect the things you value. And, like a plane, it is *extremely important*. It has to be understood, planned for, provided for. It can't fly itself.

That's what this book is all about. That's why you're holding it. If you are a living, breathing human being, you've got finances, *and they cannot be neglected*. Those who neglect their finances always live to regret it. Those who don't—they're the ones who reach their destination.

They're the ones who are happy.

The best way to reach your financial destination, I've found, is to take a leaf from a pilot's book. The best way is to *plan*.

Just as every pilot files a flight plan, so too should *every* person create a financial plan. I'll say it again: *every person should create a financial plan*. It's not just for the rich, and it's not just for the poor. It's not just for the young, and it's not just for those about to retire. It's for everyone. It's the best way to deal with the complexity; it's the best way to handle the unexpected.

So, what *is* a financial plan?

Skip the "financial" part for a second, and just look at the word "plan." A plan is a series of steps designed to help you achieve an objective. Another word for objective is "goal," and a goal is defined as a "desired result." The key word there is "desire." Our lives are built around identifying and pursuing our desires. Our desires are determined by our values. What do we truly care about? What do we *need* in order to be happy? *That* is what's at the heart of a financial plan—your values, your needs, your desires. A financial plan is a series of steps designed to help you achieve the things you care about the most.

If you follow the advice on the coming pages—gleaned from my decades of working with people just like you—then you will be able to achieve what you value most.

Now, I'm not saying this book will give you talents you don't possess or help you achieve success in your career. I'm not saying it will make you better looking or make your wildest dreams come true. I'm not even saying that everything in life has to do with finances. But the *principles* of good financial planning can extend—and be applied—to almost every facet of your life. Want a better relationship with your spouse? A financial plan can't give you one, but financial *planning* involves honesty, good communication, values, selflessness—all necessary ingredients for a successful marriage. Want to nail your dream job? A financial plan can't get it for you, but financial planning involves setting goals and figuring out what exactly you need to do to reach those goals. It involves learning how not to procrastinate. All of this has helped the most successful people in the world get to where they are today.

Again, if you're a living, breathing human being, this book is for you. As long as you are alive, you've got life ahead of you. Will you take control of the time you have left, or will it control you?

I understand that, on the surface, finances are boring. What I have tried to do with this book is create a picture that you can reflect back on, a picture that is memorable and relatable, a picture that extends beyond just your finances. That's why the word *planning* is so important—because there's not a single aspect of life that can't be improved by it.

But, of course, if you're simply looking for help in planning your finances, this book is for you, too. Whether you're interested in investments, taxes, retirement income, estate planning, or insurance, this book covers it all. What's more, I'll show you how all these topics are connected.

With that in mind, there are a few points I try to emphasize throughout this book that spell the difference between a good financial plan and a bad one. This is not take-it or leave-it advice. It's critical.

1. FINANCIAL PLANNING IS ABOUT VALUES.

The first step in creating a financial plan is deciding what you actually value in life. It's about answering these two questions: What are you doing this for? What do you care about?

There are two reasons why values are so important. The first is that unless you know what you care about, you probably won't ever take the steps to create a financial plan in the first place. People who have never thought about their values don't usually see the *need* to have a financial plan. But those who *do* know what they care about will understand how important it is to achieve or protect those things. And they will want to take every step possible to do just that.

The other reason is that for a financial plan to be successful, it must be *unique to you*. That is, it has to represent you perfectly. It shouldn't represent your planner or your neighbour or your parents. Just you. The only way for that to happen is if *your* values dictate what goes into it. People who are unhappy with their financial plan are the ones who find it doesn't truly help them with what they care about. But the reason it doesn't help them is that *they didn't put their values into the plan.* So, brace yourself because a big part of this book is about taking a long look at yourself. It's about determining who you are, what you want, and what's truly important to you. The process can be revealing.

2. A FINANCIAL PLAN HAS TO BE WRITTEN DOWN.

It may seem obvious, but a lot of folks don't get this. Just as a pilot's flight plan has to exist on paper, so too does your financial plan. It can't just be in your head. Mental plans aren't plans at all because they aren't permanent. You can't follow them exactly because there's nothing exact about them. Details will be forgotten. Aspects could change depending on your mood, the day of the week, or how many beers you've got inside you. But a plan on paper is consistent. It's immune to the shortcomings of humankind. Best of all, you can always refer to it whenever you need to.

If you don't write down your plan, you probably won't implement it. If that happens, you'll become part of somebody else's plan instead of your own.

Plus, if your plan is only in your head, it'll vanish after you die. But maybe your plan wasn't supposed to end after you die. What about the spouse you've left behind, or your children? Shouldn't they be part of your plan? Shouldn't they know it?

Of course they should. But if you die, whether it's long and slow at eighty-six or short and unexpected at forty, your plan will be for nothing unless it's written down; it's the only way your loved ones can see it.

3. YOUR PLAN WILL CHANGE.

At the same time, you should never think of your plan as being written in stone. Nothing in life is permanent because life itself isn't permanent. People change all the time. That's why your plan should evolve with you. At HSI Financial Group, we call this process the Economic Evolution. As you age, your values will change, your goals will change, and, of course, your financial situation will change. Your plan should always reflect who you are in the present, or it won't truly represent you.

Once you've got your plan down, don't think the process is over. It should be revisited on a regular basis.

(By the way, pilots don't earn their licenses and then just stop learning. We have to undergo regular, recurrent training because the industry changes over time: planes change, pilots change, and rules change. That's why we have to make sure we're always up-to-date. The same goes for you and your finances.)

4. THERE'S NO SUCH THING AS A GOOD "DO-IT-YOURSELF" PLAN.

Want to know a hard truth? Do-it-yourselfers are selfish. Here's why: do-it-yourselfers always want to be "the man" (or "the woman"). They want to be independent, the person who handles it all. Maybe they just want to save a buck. But remember, finances are *complex*. It's not nearly as simple as balancing your chequebook. So, do-it-yourselfers don't just risk getting things wrong; they'll *inevitably* get things wrong. There's just too much to know, and do-it-yourselfers don't have the time or the training to know it all.

You might think, *"So what?"* But since your finances are your own personal airplane, you rely on them to get you where you want to go. Mistakes can't be laughed off; in fact, they could be disastrous! Any given mistake could send your entire life hurtling off course.

"Again," you might say, "so what? It's my life." True, but nobody lives in a vacuum. Unless you live on a rock in the middle of the ocean, there will be people around you whose lives are affected by what you do. If *you* go hurtling off course, so do they. If you crash and burn, so do they. And if you suffer, they suffer.

That's why do-it-yourselfers are selfish. They're only thinking about themselves. They don't stop to consider the consequences to others if they screw up. That's the very definition of selfishness.

Throughout this book, I will be urging you repeatedly to hire a professional planner. It's not because I want to do my colleagues a favour. It's because it's *necessary*. Planners have the knowledge, the training, *and* the time to get things right. If you want to have a good financial plan, you *have* to have a professional help you. The point is simply not up for debate. We'll talk more about this later, but for now, just remember: don't try to do this by yourself!

Now for some good news. While personal finances are complex, this book is extremely simple. There's really nothing in here the average person couldn't understand. That's because the principles in this book are mostly common sense. In fact, some of it you'll have heard before. So, take heart: this is not difficult stuff.

One final point: you will benefit from reading this book. Unless you have all the time in the world to think about your finances, things slip through the cracks every day. Details relating to your taxes, your insurance, your wills, your investments, you name it. It never stops. This book is the first step to plugging that hole. You will see how every aspect of your finances is connected, and you will take the first steps to gaining control.

Most important, you will learn the principles of good planning. And, like every pilot knows, once you've got a plan, you can fly your plane wherever you want to go.

TWO

DON'T WASTE ANOTHER DAY

As a financial advisor, my greatest concern for *anybody* is that they have a plan. Why? Because your financial life depends on it. Think about it. Would you ever board a plane you weren't too sure about? Would you fly with a pilot who neglected to prepare and file a flight plan? Of course you wouldn't. Even if you knew the pilot—whether he or she was your parent, your cousin, or your very close friend—you still wouldn't board that plane. Your life would be at stake.

The same is true in finances. Now, people often say to me that they have plenty of friends who don't have plans, or that *they've* never had a plan, and have done very well without one. I won't argue that point. But you could say the same about flying an airplane. Sure, there have been pilots who hadn't planned ahead, who chose to "just wing it," as the expression goes. And "just winging it" might be fine when the weather is fair, the air is clear, and there's nothing else in the sky. But that rarely happens in flying, and it almost *never* happens in life.

What, then, does a plan actually look like? When pilots create a plan, they're actually looking at a map. It might be a geographical map, showing the contours of the land, how the earth rises and falls, like ripples in water. It might be a map of the airways. Regardless, pilots physically look at a map, charting how to get from point A to point B. Looking at that map, they're not just planning point to point; they're recognizing all the potential hazards along the way.

I liken those hazards to the instability of everyday life. Just as a weather forecast could hinder a pilot's progress, so too could it impact ours. When pilots contend with the weather, they look at alternate routes, alternate destinations. When they look at their map, they plan out contingencies. Where do they go if the weather turns bad? If the plane has mechanical failures? If they run out of fuel? What do they do? Any of those obstacles will impede a pilot's progress, but it's the flight plan that will overcome them. Good pilots will almost always reach their destination eventually. It's the flight plan that gets them there *safely*.

A financial plan is no different. Let me say it again: *a financial plan is no different*. A plan will get you from point A to point B. It'll help you resolve problems along the way. And it'll get you there safely.

More often than not, the people who go through life without a plan are not struggling financially day to day. Perhaps it's because those who *are* struggling know how important it is to plan; they know how easily their life can be blown off course; and they know the consequences of *not* preparing for the future.

People who have done very well for themselves, on the other hand, often don't start out with a plan. The typical attitude is, "You know, I've come this far without a plan. I'll be fine." But when turbulence hits, as it almost always does, they don't know which way to turn. It's like a pilot jerking the plane around, constantly overcompensating. When faced with misfortune, it's easy to make an ad hoc decision. And if you've ever made one of *those*, you know that it usually just leads to more trouble. People who make ad hoc decisions with their finances only compound the problem, leading to one mistake after another. This is typical of plane crashes, too. Oftentimes, the crash itself isn't due to just one problem; rather, it's from a series of problems. Usually it's because the pilot hasn't prepared, mentally or physically, for the events that can occur.

Pilots don't pick and choose which emergency procedures they have to handle. They plan for all of them. They are prepared. Once *you* have a plan, you'll be prepared, too. So, if the stock market goes down, you'll know what to do. If your spouse passes away prematurely, you'll know what to do. If you lose your job, you'll know what to do. Because you're already prepared.

Let's take a look at two different families I've known who didn't have a plan. One learned their lesson before it was too late. The other didn't.

Let's call the first couple Roger and Janet. For obvious reasons, I can't use their real names, and I've changed some of the details. But rest assured; they were a real couple with a real family who first came to visit me in the '90s. Though they are unique individuals, their story is not. I've dealt with many cases just like theirs over my career.

Roger and Janet were both in their forties. They had two young boys, ages eleven and eight. Try to picture them at this point in their lives. Try to picture their kids. It shouldn't be hard because they're probably not too different from you. Roger was a likable guy, pleasant to talk to. Janet was a stay-at-home mom, devoted to her kids and doing everything she could to make sure her family was healthy and happy. Their boys played sports when the weather was good and video-game sports when it wasn't.

Roger and Janet were at an interesting point in their lives. On the one hand, they had everything they could ask for. They had a nice home with plenty of amenities. Roger had a good job where he made $120,000 a year. Most importantly, they had each other.

On the other hand, they were just getting old enough to recognize the fragility of life. When you're young, everything important to you comes easy. As human beings, we're all wealthy at first because we're born *into* everything. Our family's been there since day one. Same with our first home. Most of our possessions are given to us. We take the good things in life for granted because we've never known it any other way.

Even when we grow up, we're still not awake to the impermanence of life. Our pursuits are usually straightforward, and the rewards from them are direct and simple to attain. They might not be *easy*, but there's a clear system of work and reward:

> ➢ If you study hard, you'll get good grades. If you get good grades, you'll get into college or university.

> If you mow lawns or deliver the paper or flip burgers in your spare time, you'll get enough money to buy that used car your neighbour is selling.

> If you are interested in someone, you ask him or her out. If you make a connection, you ask that person out again. If you fall in love, usually you'll ask him or her to marry you (or hope to get asked!). If that person says yes, you get married.

As we get older, though, our ambitions become more complicated, and the path to achieving them starts to twist. For example, it's one thing to decide to buy a house, but how many other decisions need to be made along the way? It's a lot different from shelling out a few hundred dollars to buy your neighbour's old clunker. With a house, there are mortgage loans, warranties, home owners' insurance. There's paperwork to sign, neighbourhoods to consider. Location, location, location. And even when you've bought the house, that's only the first step in a lifelong, never-ending process of actually *enjoying* it. Homes require upkeep, attention, and maintenance, in *addition* to all the unforeseen costs.

Or, what about marriage? It's easy for young people to decide they want to spend their lives together. It's much harder to actually set about doing it. For Roger and Janet, by the time they came to see me, their marriage was no longer just about being in love with each other. It was about overcoming a thousand different challenges, every day, every week, every year, to *keep* on loving each other. To not let life drive them apart. Put it this way: imagine the care, concentration, and perseverance it takes to build the world's largest card tower. Now imagine that you can't ever *stop* building it, or the whole thing will fall apart. Marriage is like that.

Life is like that.

These were the things on Roger and Janet's minds when they first came to see me. They knew how much work they'd put in to get what they had; they also knew how painful it would be if something were to take those things away.

Actually, they'd known all this for a while. But knowing something and *acting* on it are two different things. It's like making a resolution at New Years. How many people know they need to lose weight? How many people even have a desire? Of those people, how many go to the gym once and then never again? Was it really a resolution to lose weight…or just a wish?

When I'm chatting with prospective clients, I try to discover how serious they are about getting their finances in order. I divide up their wants between *goals* and *dreams*. If they're actively working towards something, it's a goal. If they're not, it's a dream or a wish or a New Year's resolution.

For Roger and Janet, planning for their future had always been just that: a wish. They knew they should do it, and they *wanted* to do it, but life kept getting in the way. They waited and waited. To be blunt, they procrastinated—until the day Roger called me and said, "We need to talk."

When they first came in, their concern was evident. They were worried about their family, about retirement, and about debt. I had concerns of my own. Neither of them had wills. There were no guardianships to take care of their children. They had very little insurance, with no disability, no critical illness, and no long-term care. They had no estate plan. In short, they had no protection. It's like boarding an airplane with no emergency exits. The parachutes aren't packed, and your seat *cannot* be used as a flotation device.

What still haunts me today is that these were people who had *everything*! A family, a house, a job. And because they had everything, *everything* was at stake. So, you can see why they were concerned. You can see why *I* was concerned.

First, we showed them what a financial plan looks like.[1] We showed them how it would get them from point A to point B, how, even if they veered off onto one of those side roads life puts in front of you, the plan could always get them back to the main road, the *right* road. But then we got to the hard part. From this moment on, I explained to Roger and Janet, everything was up to them. It was all about execution. They had their map; they had their tools. Only one thing could stop them: procrastination.

"Do you really have a burning desire to get this done?" I asked. "Are you really that concerned? Are you taking it seriously enough? Do you care about your loved ones enough to actually execute the plan?"

When we got to that point, I could see their enthusiasm starting to fade. I recognized it immediately. Roger was probably thinking, *Is this for me? Is this going to be too time-consuming?* Or, maybe Janet thought, *This is boring. It's not that exciting. I thought we were just going to talk about investing.*

---

1. For more on what a financial plan looks like, see chapters 3–5.

Maybe they were thinking, *We didn't think we would actually have to* do *something*.

We live in a world where everybody is looking for the quick fix. When the quick fix doesn't fix anything, we try to find another. It's like changing the channel to find a different weather forecast. Can you imagine flipping through news channels, trying to find a forecast that you liked? It doesn't make the problem go away. If there's a storm, there's a storm. You can't change it; all you can do is *prepare* for it. In Janet and Roger's case, their storm came sooner rather than later.

My meeting with them was on the eve of that storm. I saw them once in August and again in September. I laid everything out for them. They knew what they had to do. But after that, there was silence. We called and left messages, but we didn't hear back from them for months. When Janet called me again, it was long after.

Roger was in a coma.

He probably never thought it would happen this way. If Roger ever stopped to consider all the future events in his life, falling off his roof was probably not on the list. Nevertheless, that's all it took. Just one moment to make his family's life—that gigantic tower of cards—come crashing down.

An ambulance rushed Roger to the hospital from the site of his accident. He was badly injured—so injured, in fact, that his chance of surviving was very low. As it turns out, he *did* survive, but he'll never be the same. His brain is damaged. He can never return to work. He can never help Janet with the children.

All the concerns I had were justified. They ran into immediate cash flow problems. They had no provisions for the sort of long-term care that Roger needed. Janet had to return to full-time work just to make ends meet, which was particularly hard on the kids. Not only had they lost a full-time father, in a sense, but a full-time mother, too. How do you explain that to children?

Janet's burden didn't end there. Because they had no wills or an estate plan, Janet was forced to apply to become his legal trustee and guardian. This is not a simple process. In her case, it took quite a bit of time and quite a lot of money. First is the application to the court. Once *that* goes through, the paperwork lands on the desk of the public trustee and the public guardian. The public guardian has to give his or her stamp of approval. And there's no way of knowing just how long it will take. It could be a month. It could be two or three. It depends on the backlog in court and the backlog with the public trustee. We helped Janet through the process, but it was physically and emotionally exhausting, to say nothing of the expense. But it had to be done. With Roger incapacitated, the family couldn't so much as return a leased vehicle because Roger was the one who signed the lease.

How much of this was due to procrastination? Just about all of it. Roger and Janet are good people who've been dealt a cruel hand, but so much of the financial pain would have been alleviated if the plan had been implemented. No plan could have prevented the tragedy, but it could have helped them recover from it. In addition, we would have been there when Roger couldn't be. That's what we assure our clients: "We will be there when you can't be." If Janet had worked with us initially, it might have cost a thousand dollars to put together the wills, directives, and other documents. It cost *thousands* of dollars just for Janet to apply for guardianship.

Procrastination costs time. It costs money. If they had planned years before, Janet could have concentrated on her family rather than on paperwork. If the insurance was in place, she probably wouldn't have had to go back to work.

But it doesn't have to be this way. Let's look at a family that *didn't* procrastinate.

Bob discovered me through a public presentation I had done. After the presentation, he sat down and re-examined his life. He didn't like what he saw. For one thing, he was about seventy. For another, his life was pretty complicated, both financially and personally. In fact, you could say that a lot of his financial complications were the result of the challenges he faced in his personal life.

If you were to guess what those challenges were, you'd probably be wrong. It wasn't that his health was bad. He was a very healthy old man, the kind of person who always looks young for his age. And he was certainly well off. He'd owned a successful automotive business, and the result was that by the time he came to me, he had enough money to indulge in his passion for race cars. He even owned a few.

But there was one aspect of his life that wasn't such a success: his family. He'd divorced his first wife twenty-seven years prior and then married his second wife, Elizabeth, a few years later. He was still with Elizabeth when he met me, so obviously his second marriage had gone a bit better than the first. Still, his first marriage hung like a shadow over almost everything he did. It was a major source of stress, for Elizabeth especially.

Even more stressful were his three sons. They all had different personalities, as children usually do, but in Bob's case, they were pretty extreme personalities. Each one belonged to a different part of the spectrum. One was very controlling and rather difficult to get along with. The second was fairly passive, the kind of guy who just focuses on making ends meet. The third was a spendthrift. Since Bob was seventy, he was starting to think about what he was going to leave his family after he passed on.

When we first met, I asked him to give me a comprehensive picture of his finances. In many cases, we looked at events that were so far back in his life that he cocked his head to one side and said, "That's so far behind me; it's not an issue anymore." He was wrong, as you're about to see.

One thing he was wrong about was his divorce decree. Divorce decrees are the letters from court outlining how alimony payments work, among other things. It's understandable that he'd forgotten about it. Remember, he'd divorced his first wife over twenty years ago. But I insisted that he bring it in anyway. I said, "Just humour me. I don't know that every document in your life is still important, but when I know they exist, I look through them. I don't want to leave any stone unturned."

"Nobody has ever asked for it before," Bob said.

"Well, I am," I replied.

For our second meeting, he brought all the information I requested. He also brought Elizabeth. I had discovered some things in the meantime, so when we all sat down, I resolved that I was going to be candid with them. "You might already know some of the things we're going to talk about today," I told them, "but I'm going to talk about them anyway because I'd be remiss otherwise. I'd be *assuming* what you know, and that's a pretty dangerous thing to do."

I knew Bob had previously dealt with another financial planner, as well as with lawyers, accountants, and investment advisors. More often than not, these professionals *assume* they know certain things, so when *they* create a plan, it's not thorough. It's not detailed, nor is it very helpful because too many things are implicit. With Bob and Elizabeth, I resolved to be *explicit*.

Regarding Bob's divorce decree, he had been making those payments for so many years that he was probably just doing it on autopilot at this point. Looking at him straight on, I said, "Are you aware that your alimony payments will survive you?"

There was a little bit of hesitation. Bob didn't say anything. Elizabeth caught on quicker. She rose from her chair, her face turning red. "What you're telling me," she said, "is that I'm going to have to continue making payments? If Bob dies before me, I'm still going to have to make payments to *her*?" (In reality, her language was a bit stronger. Plainly, she had less than warm feelings for Bob's former spouse.)

"Yes, and apparently you didn't know that." She shook her head, and that set the tone for the rest of the meeting.

I had expected the same reaction from Bob. Instead, he had a little smirk on his face. Bob was a mischievous type, always looking for the humour in everything. When I asked him what he thought, he said, "Wes, I *knew* she had a better lawyer than me!" It was like a game to him. He continued to chuckle while his wife glowered. He didn't see the issue like she did because he was older, and in the end it would be *her* problem more than his. But Elizabeth couldn't stand the idea. Beyond the fact that it would continue to be a drain on their finances, she hated the idea of physically writing cheques to this other woman. Can you imagine how she would have felt if she had learned about this situation later? If no one had told her until *after* Bob died? She would have been blindsided. She would have been so furious, the anger she showed in my office would have seemed like a mild tantrum by comparison.

Here's one of the greatest things about having a plan, though. It's not only there to point out the problem. It's also there to provide you with a *solution*. I said as much to Elizabeth. "Look, the whole reason you're here is for me to find solutions. Not just problems, but solutions. I wouldn't point out a problem if I couldn't offer a solution. So, here it is. You have some old life insurance policies, one of which is one hundred percent paid for. It has cash value in it. What I want to do is use this life insurance policy as a way to solve your problem, and it won't cost you a nickel."

She sat back down in her chair, starting to calm down. I knew I had her attention. "What I'm going to do is write a trust document, or a beneficiary declaration, with this insurance policy. It'll be a one-page document. I'll send this document off to the insurance company for their approval. Here's what it will say. If Bob dies before you or dies before his former spouse, to whom you're paying alimony, the insurance company will go ahead and make the payments to her *directly* every month. That way, you'll no longer have to write cheques to her; instead, it'll come out of this life insurance policy, not out of your regular income. Then, when *she* dies, the balance of the policy will be left over for you."

Elizabeth was brightening by the second, but she still had concerns. "You said it wouldn't cost us a nickel to do this. How do you figure?"

"Because I'm not going to charge you anything extra for doing it. You're paying me for this plan, and it's included *in the plan.* Part of a plan is identifying problems. The other part is coming up with solutions. As far as I'm concerned, when you pay me for one part, you're paying for the whole thing. What do you think?"

She looked at Bob and then back at me. "We love it," she said. "Make it happen."

What's really interesting is that Bob had already visited a fee-only financial planner whom he was referred to by his bank manager, and his recommendation was to cancel the insurance policy—the very thing we used to solve the alimony problem. And equally as important, he missed the alimony problem altogether.

Next we covered Bob's estate plan. For the most part, it was nonexistent. This is where his kids came into the picture. What was he going to leave for them? What were they going to do with it? Remember, these were three very different people, one of which was a spendthrift, a gambler, and an alcoholic to boot. Every time this particular son got money, it was gone the next day. "Still," I pointed out, "he's your son, and you love him."

Bob agreed. "The thing is," he said, "if I give him a quarter of my estate all at once"—he also had a daughter with Elizabeth—"then he'll be dead in a few days." He was worried that his son would go crazy with all that money, drinking or gambling it away, and get into more trouble than he could handle, in which case the money wouldn't be a blessing; it would be a curse.

I explained to him how we would model his estate plan so that it was good for everybody. It wouldn't be just about divvying up his money. It would be about ensuring his family was *taken care of* after he was gone. We went through each child separately, determining each personality and what he or she would need because of those personalities. Although Bob wanted to treat all his children equally, he quickly realized this wouldn't be possible. Sometimes, people have to be protected from themselves.

Bob was incredulous. "We can do that?"

"Absolutely, we can do that," I replied. "It's not a problem. It's what we do."

We decided that his third son, the spendthrift, would be given payouts on a regular basis—enough to help, but not enough to harm, and enough to live on, but not enough to die from. You see, I was not prepared to just sit down with Bob and say, "OK, we're going to just give money to all your children equally, and we'll name a trustee, and that's it. Thanks for coming." That's a pretty impersonal way of doing business, and really, it's not a plan. A plan is taking things on an individual basis. A plan takes into consideration your thoughts, your feelings, and your emotions.

By this point, Bob and Elizabeth were pretty much sold. They were seeing firsthand how the plan wasn't just pointing out problems, but providing solutions. They set to work implementing the plan, and everything went along quite nicely. Bob recognized that time was not on his side, but in the end, because they devised a plan, and because they *implemented* that plan, all the problems they might not have even seen coming were already taken care of.

In the end, they knew they could reach their destination.

KNOW YOU CAN

Whether you're flying a plane or walking through everyday life on your own two feet, you have to have a destination in mind. Either way, you're going to run into obstacles. You'll hit some turbulence, and unexpected events will knock you off course. Pilots know to plan for those sorts of things. The result is that each day, tens of thousands of planes take off and land safely, all around the world.

But on the ground? That's where the accidents happen.

I've seen far more people crash and burn their financial lives—and by extension, their personal lives, too—than I've seen pilots crash their airplanes. It's a valuable lesson that I hope I've made clear. If you're still not convinced, ask around. Talk to your friends, your family. Find out who has a plan. Ask that person if he or she has any regrets.

While a plan can't prevent tragedy, it can help you *recover* from tragedy. It can help *protect* you from it. Roger and Janet learned that lesson too late.

A plan can also identify potential problems before they become serious problems. Bob and Elizabeth had no idea they'd be paying money to another woman long after Bob was gone. If it wasn't for the plan, they might have never known—at least, not until the event took place.

A good plan also provides *solutions*. It's not enough to see storm clouds on the horizon. You also have to know what you're going to *do* about them. In Bob and Elizabeth's case, a plan provided solutions that they never knew were possible—solutions to fix his alimony problem or to take care of his troubled children. The point is *they didn't* know until the plan showed them. I'm sure you've heard the phrase, "Knowing is half the battle." It's true. I'd even suggest that knowing is planning. So, in your fight to ensure a stable retirement or a healthy financial future, *planning* is half the battle.

By the way, some people procrastinate because they're afraid. They put off working with a planner because they're afraid what their plan might reveal. If you ever feel afraid, remember: a planner's job is not to judge but to help. That's why good planners get into the business in the first place: they want to help. If you work with a planner and you feel judgment taking place, you shouldn't work with that planner. But if you choose your planner wisely (we'll cover this more in chapter 6), then you won't have to worry. You don't have to be afraid.

Don't let fear lead to procrastination. Having a financial plan will replace that fear with knowledge—the knowledge that you *can* protect yourself from life's obstacles, that you *can* find solutions to your problems. Don't put off reaching your destination because you're afraid. With a financial plan, you'll know you can reach it. When a problem develops, you will be prepared to handle it—with confidence.

I've learned in life that if something's worth doing, it's worth doing right. And if you aren't doing it right, you'll usually end up not doing it at all. So, we might as well be frank and say that if you're not serious about having a plan, you're not really serious about getting to your destination. There's not a pilot in the world who can *consistently* and *safely* get you to where you want to be without a plan. There's not a traveler in the world who would ever leave home without one. If you're serious, truly serious about reaching your financial goals, then don't waste another day.

Make a plan. Start now. Throughout the next several chapters, I'll show you what your plan should look like, and how to *know you can* create one.

THREE

CREATING A PLAN, PART I

When a pilot flies a plane, his or her flight plan is always available. That way, it can be referenced at any time. The plan can be in a number of formats. Some pilots still use the old paper format. Some have their plan programmed into an iPad. And there's always a backup hardwired into the plane. The point is, no matter what format the pilot chooses, it's *always* there, ready to be called upon. It's not just in the pilot's head; it's physical, tangible, something the pilot can feel and touch.

Your financial plan should be the same way. You should be able to see it, touch it. You should be able to refer to it at any time. Suddenly lose your job? The plan will tell you what to do next. Is there a critical illness in the family? Check your plan to determine how to handle it. Faced with a troubled stock market or investment? The plan will guide you. It sounds incredible, but this is why you have a plan. This is what a plan *is*. It's a roadmap, a blueprint. Pick whatever synonym you want, and you've got it with your plan.

But your plan needs to be a physical thing, whether printed on paper or uploaded digitally to some device. Ideas that exist only in your head tend to change. They get distorted. But ideas with physical form are concrete. They're reliable. There's a reason why we don't base our self-image off what we see in our dreams. We base it off what we see in the mirror. The mirror is reliable and consistent. Dreams are not.

If your plan is written down, if it's specific to *you*, if it's comprehensive and step-by-step, you should be able to hand it to any financial professional with the confidence that he or she can execute it. For example, maybe you don't want the planner you worked with to be the one who actually implements the plan. Maybe you have a specific investment advisor in mind. Regardless, you should be able to say, "Here's my plan; this is what I want you to do." And they should do it. It's that simple. If you take your plan to any three financial advisors, it should come out the same for each of them. Sure, there may be different *interpretations*, but the end result should be the same. It's like handing a roadmap to three different drivers. The map starts in Calgary and ends up in Vancouver, but the three drivers might make different rest stops along the way. They may drive some sections faster and some slower, but they'll all end up in the same place, around the same time.

As you work with your planner, ask him or her to physically show you the plan. Always make sure you can see it.

So far in this book, we've discussed why you need a plan and why it's important not to procrastinate. Now, let's go over what a plan should actually look like.

I've worked in this business for twenty-eight years. During that time, I've honed and perfected a sample plan that I show to prospective clients when we first meet. The sample illustrates all the various aspects of your life that need to be planned for. The plan *your* planner comes up with won't necessarily look the same, but it should probably be close. Although it might be a different format or a different structure, it should address all the same topics, and with the same level of detail. As you work through the process of choosing a planner, ask to see a sample plan. If the planner can't (or won't) provide one, walk away. Once you have seen a sample plan, compare it to mine. Again, two plans won't look exactly the same, but they should be similar. Obviously, I can't include an actual plan with this book, but in the next three chapters, you'll learn about all the different things that can and should go into a financial plan. Compare these chapters to your planner's sample plan. Most planners won't release the sample plan to you. You just want to review it in their office with them so you know what you can expect.

In my case, I use a binder. Each tab in my binder corresponds to one of the life aspects previously mentioned. Remember, every tab *together* is what makes a real plan. A planner who focuses on just one or two of these—and ignores the others—should send up red flags. For example, many so-called financial plans are just weak investment plans. Don't confuse these with a real financial plan. A real plan would *include* an investment plan, but it should give equal weight to all the other aspects of your finances as well. That's because these aspects complement each other. When you improve one, you can improve them all.

The tabs I use are labeled like this:

- Meeting Agenda

- Critical Financial Events

- Personal Financial Policy Statement

- Tax Planning

- Retirement Planning

- Cash Flow Planning

- Educational Savings

- Your Family's Security

- Estate Planning—Personal

- Estate Planning—Business

- Investment Strategies

We use these tabs for every plan we create. It's our checklist to make sure we've completed a *thorough* plan for every client. Think of it as a recipe. If people follow this recipe, they're going to end up with a pretty good product at the other end. It'll be tasty and pleasing. We know that because we've tested it and refined it and updated it over three decades.

Note also that the investment plan is last on the list. We don't tackle investments until we identify our clients' needs. Doctors don't write a prescription until they've given you a diagnosis, right? To do otherwise would be malpractice. It's no different for us, and it should be no different with your financial plan.

To help you understand exactly what should go *into* a financial plan, let's do a brief run-through of each tab.

MEETING AGENDA

Every time a client comes in for a meeting, we provide them with an agenda. The agenda includes notes from our last meeting, a summary of the paperwork signed or given, plus an itinerary for our current meeting. This is helpful for clients because it keeps them engaged. It helps them know *exactly* where we are in the planning process. Plus, it allows them to refer back and remember what we discussed last time. Whether our relationship lasts two years or twenty, clients can use these agendas as a kind of measuring stick to gauge their progress. That's why we *always* provide an agenda, for every client, every time. It's a powerful tool.

When you work with your planner, ask him or her to provide some kind of agenda, or at least the minutes from your previous meeting, so that you can prepare for the next one. This way, you'll see every step of the process in the context of your overall plan.

CRITICAL FINANCIAL EVENTS

Two things you should know:

1. Critical Financial Events affect your finances, either now or in the future. These events include retiring, planning for a child's education, getting a raise, or losing a job.

2. Critical Financial Events are *going* to happen. Period. Accept this now, and let's get it out of the way. You might go your whole life without ever experiencing a natural disaster. You might never get in a car crash. But *no one* goes through life without experiencing multiple Critical Financial Events. So, instead of trying to avoid them, *plan* for them, especially because some Critical Financial Events are good!

Some Critical Financial Events are predictable, but they can often be random and unexpected. Again, "critical" does not necessarily mean "catastrophic." But in case it does, we plan for those here, too. This section of the plan, then, is about *identifying* potential events and then deciding how your financial goals will dictate your response. In fact, there's a case to be made that Critical Financial Events are the single best reason to have a plan. When you work with your planner, make sure you identify the possible events in *your* life so you can plan for them.

How you deal with Critical Events is just as important as recognizing them. There's a right way and a wrong way. Identifying and planning is the right way. Making knee-jerk decisions is the wrong way. In fact, sometimes we turn simple things *into* catastrophic events because we panic and make knee-jerk decisions. If a pilot panics when a problem occurs, it usually leads to disaster. Instead of taking simple, elementary steps to deal with it, the pilot starts jerking around and making things worse.

The same is true in finances. I'll give an example. Say you're planning a vacation. Simple, right? You wouldn't consider it a big decision to go on vacation. But how are you going to pay for it?

The smart thing to do would be to set money aside so you can pay for your vacation. You want to make sure you can afford it, right? So, include in your plan that you want to travel. That way, you can say, "OK, this is how much money I owe in taxes, and this is how much money I owe to the bank, and I'll have *this* much money by this date. Can I go on vacation or not?" If the answer is yes, great. If the answer is *no,* then determine how much money you *do* need that isn't already earmarked for something else. Once you have the amount, you can adjust many other things in order to come up with it. You can choose to save more a month, for example. You can choose to pay down your debt quicker. Or, you can choose to work some extra hours. What's more, you can determine *how much* should be saved a month or *how quickly* you can pay down your debt or *how many* extra hours you'll need to work.

That's your plan for going on vacation. When the time comes, you'll have the money to pay for it. You can get on a plane, enjoy the sun, and come back with pictures, memories, and no regrets at all.

Or you can just wing it.

Again, say you're planning a vacation. Simple, right? It's not a big decision to go on vacation. But how are you going to pay for it?

The not-so-smart thing to do would be to just put it all on your credit card. So, off you go, racking up charges all the way. When you get home, you find out that you've maxed out your card, incurring penalties. Plus, your interest rate is high. Before you know it, the vacation that should have cost only $10,000 is costing you $25,000. Even worse, your credit score goes down. So, if bad luck strikes and your car gets totaled a few months later, you now have $15,000 less to buy a new one. You can't get a loan because your credit score isn't good enough, and without a car, you can't get to work, so you get fired.

"What just happened?" you wail. "All I did was go on vacation!"

Sure. But you also had a Critical Financial Event, and because you didn't plan for it, that Critical Event became a catastrophic one. That's why pilots always plan for the worst, and it's why you should, too.

PERSONAL FINANCIAL POLICY STATEMENT

In the previous chapter, I said that one of the most important things a planner can do is find out what's important to you—to learn what you truly care about and then plan accordingly. Your plan should help protect the things you value most; it should help you acquire the things you most desire; and it should give you peace of mind. But the only way a plan can do that is if the planner learns about *you*.

In my sample plan, the Personal Financial Policy Statement is the first step I take to learning what my client cares about. There are three documents every client must fill out. The first is what we call an Economic Evolution Scorecard. A sample scorecard is shown below.

I/We do not have a clear vision of my/our future	1	2	3	4	5	6	7	8	9	10	I/We have a clear, well-defined vision of my/our future
I/We do not have clear financial goals	1	2	3	4	5	6	7	8	9	10	I/We have clear financial goals
I/We feel I/we are flying blind, both financially and personally in my/our life	1	2	3	4	5	6	7	8	9	10	I/We feel I/we have a clear vision and flight path for the future
I/We are worried and anxious about my/our financial future	1	2	3	4	5	6	7	8	9	10	I/We feel confident and relaxed about my/our financial future
I/We have not developed strategies to achieve my/our financial goals	1	2	3	4	5	6	7	8	9	10	I/We have developed strategies to achieve my/our financial goals
My/Our plan and strategies are not evolving with changing circumstances	1	2	3	4	5	6	7	8	9	10	My/Our plan and strategies evolve with changing circumstances
I/We am/are not confident that I/we will fully enjoy my/our retirement	1	2	3	4	5	6	7	8	9	10	I/We have a plan to fully protect and provide for my/our family's future
I/We am/are not sure if I/we have fully protected, or provided for my/our family's future	1	2	3	4	5	6	7	8	9	10	I/We have a plan to fully protect and provide for my/our family's future
I/We am/are not confident about the advice and support I/we am/are receiving	1	2	3	4	5	6	7	8	9	10	I/We am/are extremely happy and confident about the advice I/we am/are receiving
I/We am/are concerned about losing my/our wealth	1	2	3	4	5	6	7	8	9	10	I/We am/are confident that I/we will protect and grow my/our wealth during my/our lifetime and beyond

Your Economic Evolution Scorecard Total: _____

Filling out this scorecard will help you clarify your current situation. Which aspects of your financial life need the most work? Which aspects need the least? If a client circles the number 2 next to "I do not have clear financial goals," then I know that our first task is to create some. You cannot plan for *anything* in life without goals. Goals are the destination in every journey. Author Zig Ziglar said, "A goal properly set is halfway reached." Goals give *purpose* to our lives. In many ways, they're what separate humans from animals. Most animals live by instinct, going from moment to moment, looking only to satisfy their immediate needs, whereas human beings set goals. That's why we have the capacity to plan; we envision such concepts as "tomorrow" and "the future." Setting goals helps us choose what we want the *most*, as opposed to what we want *right now*.

If a client circles an eight, then I know we don't really have to worry about that. The goals are already there. But what about *achieving* those goals? If a client circles a four next to "I have not developed strategies to achieve my financial goals," then creating those strategies is exactly what we'll do.

Occasionally I'll get clients who don't take the scorecard seriously. I'll know right away because they'll circle all nines and tens. Clients who do that are usually the ones who are most afraid. They're afraid to tell the truth. They're afraid to even *face* the truth. Some are simply afraid of being judged. But, remember, the planner isn't there to judge you. He or she is there to *help* you. Others might think, "If I circle a low number, what does that say about me?" Or, "I'm a well-educated person, so my scorecard should be all nines and tens." Well, no it shouldn't. This isn't a personality test. No one's *born* with clear goals or strategies or a plan for retirement. It's not like these things come naturally. You have to *work* at it. So, you'd *expect* some of those numbers to be low because the only way they'd be up is if you *already had a plan*. And if you already had a plan (assuming it's a good one), then why are you even meeting with me?

Ultimately, it's easy to see through the charade. You say you have clear financial goals? OK, show them to me. You have a clear financial plan? Where is it? Have you written it down? You're confident about your retirement? Great—now tell me *why*. Of course, clients usually can't. It's a sobering moment, but it's also a really important one; it helps them come to terms with reality. Once that happens, we can finally start turning those *twos* into *tens*.

The scorecard also monitors your progress. For instance, when prospective clients first come to see me, they might circle a six next to "We feel we have a clear vision and flight path for the future." Well, what about a year after? What about when the plan's been created? Are they happy with the plan? Is it providing them with both the direction and peace of mind they were looking for? If they come back to see me and circle a five, well, then obviously we didn't do a very good job. In fact, apparently we made things worse. But moving from a six to a seven—or a six to an eight—is progress. It also helps *me* determine whether we're actually talking about the right things.

I also have my clients answer the following questions:

1. What are your greatest concerns about your current situation (financial, professional, and personal) that cause you to lose sleep at night?

2. What do you like most about your current situation (financial, professional, and personal)?

3. What do you like least about your current situation (financial, professional, and personal)?

4. What roadblocks currently stand in your way to achieving your goals?

5. What are the most important actions you must take to overcome the roadblocks to reach success?

6. What actions do you need to take first?

7. Are you committed to achieving these goals?

8. People who do business with HSI Financial Group respect and value our advice. Do you feel that a properly constructed plan—unique to your situation that solves any problems or pains you've experienced—would be beneficial? (We got this one from author Dan Sullivan, founder of "The Strategic Coach" program.)

And now the really big question:

9. What is the most important thing to you in this world, personally and financially?

When our clients answer these questions, we can determine what brought them to us in the first place. What prompted their initial desire to ever speak with a planner? What do they love most? What do they fear the most? If we can address *these* issues, then we'll have achieved the most fundamental purpose of planning.

I said it in the last chapter: your planner *has* to find out what's important to you. The questions above give us a quick, easy snapshot, but we go deeper. Your planner should, too.

Simply put, I'm talking about *values*.

This is where the rubber meets the road. We want to find out exactly *what's important* and *how important it is to you.* In our plan, we do a values analysis of each client. It's like making a list of all the things you'd save during a natural disaster. What's on that list? The unique stuff, the stuff that's irreplaceable. What order do you save it in? What do you save *first?* Hopefully your kids, if you have any, and then yourself or your significant other. Pets come after that, and so on.

Then, combine that list with a different one. Maybe it's your list of goals. Some people call it a bucket list. What do you want to achieve? What do you admire in others?

For example, *my* plan would show that I have a high regard for scholastic pursuits. I place a *big* premium on education, both for myself and my children. From the day I got out of high school, I've made sure that I never stop learning. I don't stop asking questions. I don't stop taking courses. If I did, I would die inside. So, my plan *has to factor that in.* It has to allow me the time and the money to keep learning. If it didn't, the plan would be a failure because *I* would feel like a failure, plain and simple.

What are *your* values? My plan has 'em. Yours should, too.

Here are just a few of the values we ask our clients about. Each one is ranked on a scale from one to ten, with one being "Not Important" and ten being "Very Important."

- **Academics** – Do you value continuing education?

- **Achievement** – What do you want to be remembered for?

- **Adventure** – Do you try things in new and interesting ways?

- **Enjoyment** – How important is it to just have fun?

- **Family** – Do you care for and contribute to your kin?

- **Personality** – How important is it for you to have your life carefully planned?

I cannot stress enough how crucial this all is. These values create a *unique, specific, properly weighted* plan. They affect not only the style of the plan, but the nuts and bolts, too. For instance, you probably didn't realize that knowing your values is the first step to picking suitable investments. There's plenty more that goes into it, of course, but remember, when choosing investments, it's crucial that you pick the right ones for *you*. Not the right ones for Warren Buffett or your brother or anyone else. Just you. That's what you see, more often than not, when people start talking about bad investments. There's usually nothing wrong with the *investment*. That's like saying there's something wrong with a style of music. It's that the investment wasn't right for them.

For example, say you mark on the scorecard that you're afraid of losing your wealth. Let's also say that on the list of values, you put a ten next to "Security." Well, obviously, getting into an extremely speculative investment isn't going to be the right thing for you. In fact, it could be a disaster. However, that doesn't mean the investment itself is bad; it may well be a *great* investment for someone else. It simply didn't fit what *you* want, what *you* value. Discovering what you care about can be the difference between investments that make you and investments that break you.

As you work with your planner, make sure you discuss your values *first*. Everything else comes after. In short, values give your plan a purpose. Just as you can't pull a cart without a horse, you can't have a plan without a purpose.

TAX PLANNING

Would you believe it if I said that, for most people, tax planning is never done?

Too often we confuse "tax planning" and "tax preparation." The terms are not interchangeable. A tax plan is just that: a plan for your taxes. With a tax plan, you're looking ahead, determining what your taxes are going to look like. Tax preparation, on the other hand, is merely compiling the numbers on the taxes you've already paid.

To put it simple: tax planning equals future. Tax preparation equals past.

While your plan should have a section devoted to planning your taxes, be wary: too many institutions, planners, and investment advisors all run ads trying to lure you in with the promise of lower tax rates. It's an easy hook because everybody hates taxes, right?

Quite frankly, I have a different outlook. By paying taxes, I'm doing my part as a citizen. Furthermore, if I'm paying more tax, I must be making more money. On the flip side, if I'm not paying any tax, I'm probably not making any money (at least, not *legal* money).

Now, that doesn't mean we want to be overly patriotic either. Nobody, including me, wants to pay more than what they really owe. We just want to pay our fair share. We want to legally take advantage of any tax break we can get. We want to abate as much tax as possible. That's what a tax plan does. It's more than just finding a few random deductions here and there; it's about knowing ahead of time exactly how much we're going to pay so that we can plan the rest of our finances accordingly. Think how liberating that is! It takes away so much guesswork. Now you won't have to *speculate* how much you'll have left after taxes; you'll *know*. That means you'll *know* what you can do with the rest of your money and what you can't. Even better, you'll know if you need to do things differently in the future.

Again, though, be wary of the hook. For example, some institutions will use the hook that if you put your money into an investment that pays out dividends, you can reduce your taxes by 50 percent or more. (The thinking is that if you get paid solely in dividends, you won't pay any tax on the investment.) That's a terrible, terrible message to send. People often say to me, "You know, my other guy told me that, and I'm getting dividends, but I'm still paying tax." Why? Because there's a lot more to the story than what some professionals are telling you.

The thing about a hook isn't that it's a lie. It's actually true. But it might not be true *for you*. I keep coming back to this point: everything that happens in life, whether it's financially related or not, is unique to the person experiencing it. People might have common experiences or related backgrounds or similar situations, but *they're not identical*. That's true for taxes as well. Yes, there are rules, guidelines, terms, and so on, but you can't draw neat little lines around everything. Not everybody fits into the same box.

So, if someone promises you an investment that only pays dividends and doesn't get taxed, be careful. Ask, "Who does this investment apply to? Does it apply to me? What's the fine print?" Otherwise, you might come back to your planner and say, "Well, gee whiz, I'm getting these dividends, but I'm still paying taxes." The planner's response will be, "Well, yeah, but there was this item on your tax return that negated what I said." Why didn't anyone look at that *before* you chose the investment?

A proper tax plan ensures that never happens. It coordinates your taxes with everything else in your financial picture. It lets you know ahead of time so you can make the right decisions for *your* situation, not somebody else's.

Ultimately, be very careful of any tax advice you get. Make sure your planner takes into account how your taxes impact other parts of the plan, and vice versa. And remember: tax planning and tax preparation are not the same thing. Only the former controls your future.

KNOW YOU CAN

Hopefully you're starting to see some of the ways a plan can improve your financial life and create more peace of mind. With a financial plan, you'll know you can manage and overcome the inevitable Critical Financial Events in your life. You'll know, too, that you can go on vacation when you want to and where you want to. You'll know you're not paying too much in taxes. Most important, you'll know you can attain the things you value most—because the plan will show you how.

In the next chapter, we'll discuss some other sections of our sample plan.

FOUR

CREATING A PLAN, PART II

In this chapter, we'll continue with the various elements that go into a financial plan.

RETIREMENT PLANNING

Most people can't tell the difference at first between a retirement plan and a financial plan. But it's very simple. A retirement plan is just one facet of your overall financial plan. Like your overall financial plan, everybody's retirement plan is different. There's no cookie-cutter approach to retirement, so your retirement plan should be specific to you. We'll talk about retirement planning throughout the book, but for now, we'll just cover the basics.

As with financial planning in general, the main step of retirement planning is determining what's important to you. What do you want to get out of retirement? What are your dreams? What are your requirements? What do you want to know you can do? Only then can we plan out what you'll actually *need* for retirement. Once you have that plan, you'll *know* you can retire. You'll also know *when* you can retire, which is just as important.

First, though, you *must* have a picture in your head about what retirement looks like. There are many different ways of looking at that picture. Maybe you have a visual image in your mind: you see yourself in good health, surrounded by grandchildren, on a beach somewhere. Maybe you see yourself on the golf course. Maybe you see yourself doing volunteer work. It could be almost anything.

Or maybe you want to look at it graphically. Some people just want to look at numbers. Frankly, that's what I see too often. People will go to a planner or a bank and ask for retirement help, not really knowing what to expect. They haven't decided what's important to them, and they're not told to. So, when they get their plan back, it's basically a report. It doesn't reflect their values or their goals, but holy cats it's got graphs, numbers, and charts (in both pie and bar form, no less!).

It's not that these visual aids aren't helpful—they can be. But numbers should never be the center of your retirement plan. Rather, they should be indicators of how close or far away you are from your goals. They should always be expressed in real, practical terms—that is, "X is my goal; Y is how much I already have towards that goal; and Z is how much I need to get to that goal." For example, say you buy a cabin. It doesn't matter when you buy it, even if you're only forty. A good retirement plan should be able to reflect how much money you spent on the cabin, how it affects what you need to save, and what expenses it will create after you retire. A good plan will also help you determine *why* you are buying the cabin, whether it's for family events, for your kids to use, for renting, what have you. There could be a number of different reasons, but those reasons could change after you retire. Maybe you stop using the cabin or you don't have the health to use it, and in retrospect, it would have made more sense just to rent a cabin instead of buying one. Creating a plan will help you determine the *value* of what you're doing, and whether it fits with what you really want. A financial plan is about more than just dollars and cents; it's about determining what you truly value. It will also help you to make adjustments as need be as in the case of buying a cabin—or, at the very least, open it up for discussion.

Basically, a retirement plan should list your expenses after retirement and the money you will need to *pay* for those expenses. Then, it should list your *goals* after retirement and the money you'll need *after* expenses to reach those goals. Your goals prior to retirement are important, too, because those goals could affect the variables in your retirement plan. Finally, it should have suggestions for how much you should earn and save, based on a schedule, as you approach retirement. For instance, the plan should indicate how much money you should set aside per paycheque in order to cover your expenses.

But first thing's first. Once your planner knows what's important to you, he or she can sit down and draft an actual analysis of how close you are to retirement. Here's what my analysis might look like:

CREATING A PLAN, PART II | 41

| Economic Evolution Financial Analysis | Bill & Mary Smith |

Retirement Analysis

Planning Options

Your retirement situation:
Based on your goals, the information you have provided and the assumptions used in this analysis...

You are projected to have less assets than you will need to fund your retirement.

Your financial situation offers you a number of planning options:

Option #1: Reduce Lifestyle — $54,100 after-tax income starting at age 60

Amount by which you will need to reduce your retirement income: $11,900

$54,100

Base retirement income assuming no additional savings: $43,000 | After-tax retirement income goal: $68,000

Option #2: Work Longer — $66,000 after-tax income starting at age 66

Number of years you will need to continue working beyond your planned retirement age: 6

Age 60

Your age on January 1st: 44 | Age you will be able to afford to retire: 66

Option #3: Earn More Return — $66,000 after-tax income starting at age 60

Average annual increase in Return on Investment needed to reach your goals: 2.42%

ROR 4.89%

Inflation adjusted rate of return: 1.44% | Return on Investment you need to earn: 7.31%

Option #4: Save More — $66,000 after-tax income starting at age 60

Additional amount you will need to save each year to reach your goals: $24,000

$857,000

Current value of retirement investments: $170,000 | Capital needed at your retirement: $1,507,000

The planning options presented are based on numerous assumptions that are certain to change and cannot be guaranteed. Actual results will vary over the life of your plan.

Figure 1. Retirement Analysis.

(In case it's hard to read, the fine print at the bottom says, "The planning options presented are based on numerous assumptions that are certain to change and cannot be guaranteed. Actual results will vary over the life of your plan." This is why we always *implore* our clients to do a review regularly. It's critical to the success of their plan. Investments change, the economy changes, our clients change, you name it. Life doesn't stand still, and neither do your finances. It's a constant process of economic evolution.)

This graphic was done with a software program by *FPAdvantage*, and it was reproduced with their permission. We, like everybody else, use computers as a tool to help calculate the numbers that go into a financial plan. Normally, the graphs and charts we use are printed in colour, with an accompanying legend so that our clients can interpret what each colour means. When writing this book, however, I determined not to use colour graphics, because I don't want you to get hung up on how each chart looks. The planner you work with might use different software, different colours, or different formatting, and I don't want you to read your financial plan with a preconceived notion of what the graphics should look like.

The samples provided here are just an illustration of some of the components that make up a good financial plan. Software is not a plan; it's really just an elaborate calculator. It's useful, but it still needs an operator. Just as a piece of wood is not a chair, a piece of software is not a financial plan.

In this case, our hypothetical clients, Bill and Mary Smith, aren't currently able to fund the retirement they had in mind. You can see that near the top, where it says, "You are projected to have less assets than you will need to fund your retirement." But it's no reason to get upset. How much better is it for Bill and Mary to know this *now* rather than later? Knowing *now* means you can do something about it. Knowing later means you can't. Once Bill and Mary see they *can't* fund their retirement, they can explore solutions. By proper planning, they'll *know they can* fund their retirement, as opposed to simply hoping they can.

By the way, I didn't mention Bill's and Mary's age. That's because it doesn't matter. Your retirement plan should also show how much money you can spend when you're young and healthy, long before you quit working. You don't have to be in your fifties or sixties to get value out of this. While your age *will* affect your options, you don't have to be a certain age to start preparing for retirement.

As you can see from the graphic, if your planner's analysis indicates you don't have the means to fund your retirement, then your plan should include suggestions on how to rectify that. This is really where your planner earns his or her keep. Your planner is more than a calculator. He or she should be able to help show you different options, choices, and alternate routes to your destination. Again, your planner's suggestions should be expressed in real terms. For instance, if Bill and Mary want to fund their retirement, they might consider the following:

- *Lowering their retirement income needs*. This ultimately involves adjusting their expectations. If Bill and Mary Smith want to tour the country in a motorhome *and* buy a boat, then maybe they should consider dropping the boat.

- *Working longer*. Based upon how much they're currently earning and how much they still need, Bill and Mary will need to work six years longer than what they had planned.

- *Getting a higher return*. This refers to Bill and Mary's investments. If they chose this route, they would be looking to adopt more risk in order to accumulate more reward. This may or may not be a good idea; if I were their planner, I would recommend it only if I felt it appropriate. Generally speaking, a good financial planner should err on the side of caution, emphasizing what's realistic over what's possible. A prudent person never bets on his or her retirement, and gambling on a higher rate of return is never prudent.

- *Saving more.* Based upon their projections, Bill and Mary would need to save an extra $2,000 a month to fund their retirement, or $65 a day.

The most realistic course of action is to combine some of these options. For instance, they could increase their savings, work an extra year or two, *and* cut a couple of the luxuries they had hoped to enjoy. It's a lot easier to partially implement multiple options than fully implement a single one.

Whatever they decide to do, the important thing is that we used both their financials *and* their values to create this analysis. Now they actually have a *plan*, not just a wing and a prayer. They know exactly what they want and exactly how to get it. Your plan should do the same for you.

One other note: it's important to keep in mind that you should be regularly adjusting the numbers in your plan based on the goals you want to accomplish in your life. Your goals at thirty-five might not be the same at fifty. You'll probably have different values as you get older. Charity work might mean little to you when you have a family to take care of, but once you're left with an empty nest? Charity might be the only thing that makes you feel good. You never know. So, as *you* change, so should the numbers in your retirement plan.

Ultimately, your plan, be it financial or retirement, should be dynamic. That's why my personal financial planning process is called the Economic Evolution Program. The entire world is constantly evolving, and you're evolving with it. But whatever your planner calls it, with a plan, you'll *know you can* retire, and you'll know what you need to do to get there.

CASH FLOW PLANNING

Cash flow planning, in a lot of ways, is the nitty-gritty part of your plan. We've talked about how so much of financial planning isn't just graphs; it isn't just charts. It's finding out what you value in life. But at some point, it's necessary to figure out how to *pay* for those values. The Cash Flow section of the plan is the first step. Basically, it's how we track how much money you have coming in and how much you've got going out—not just now, but twenty years from now, too.

This is where we crunch the numbers. After you've determined what you want in life, what you *need*, and how important it is to you, we figure out how much all of it is going to cost. How much are you spending on necessities now? How much are you likely to spend in the future? How much are you spending on luxuries now?

This is how cash flow fits within your overall plan: what we do is look at your current sources of income—investments, employment, Registered Retirement Savings Plans (RRSPs), and so on—as well as your expenses, such as how much tax you're paying. Then we'll try to project what your income and expenses will look like every year for the next several decades, all the way up until you're well into retirement. We'll balance that against what your income needs to be in order for you to reach your goals. So, for instance, if you're depositing so much a year, and your investments make so much a year, but you're withdrawing money at so much a year, what will your income needs be? Are you earning enough? If you're not, what will the picture look like if you increase the amount you save each year? How much should that increase be? What kind of a return will your investments have to generate? Or, if you had a large expenditure one year, how would that affect your plan?

CREATING A PLAN, PART II | 45

Economic Evolution Planning Analysis — Bill & Mary Smith

Projected Cash Flow

Values are estimated based on an after-tax income goal in retirement of $60,000 in today's dollars

	Year	B	M	Investment Savings	RRSP RRIF	Cash Investments	Other Income	Income Goal	Excess (Deficiency)	Income Tax	Paid by Withholding	Paid From Investment*	Paid From Cash Flow
						Sources of Income					Income Tax		
1	2011	45	42	19,000	0	0	130,000	0	0	(25,901)	0	0	25,901
2	2012	46	43	19,475	0	0	133,250	0	0	(26,548)	0	0	26,548
3	2013	47	44	19,962	0	0	136,581	0	0	(27,212)	0	0	27,212
4	2014	48	45	20,461	0	0	139,996	0	0	(27,892)	0	0	27,892
5	2015	49	46	20,972	0	0	143,496	0	0	(28,590)	0	0	28,590
6	2016	50	47	21,497	0	0	147,083	0	0	(29,304)	0	0	29,304
7	2017	51	48	22,034	0	0	150,760	0	0	(30,037)	0	0	30,037
8	2018	52	49	22,585	0	0	154,529	0	0	(30,788)	0	0	30,788
9	2019	53	50	23,150	0	0	158,392	0	0	(31,558)	0	0	31,558
10	2020	54	51	23,728	0	0	162,352	0	0	(32,346)	0	0	32,346
16	2026	60	57	0	15,994	43,844	27,060	86,898	0	(1,116)	2,172	0	(1,056)
17	2027	61	58	0	16,810	40,842	31,418	89,070	0	(2,197)	2,209	0	(12)
18	2028	62	59	0	17,693	41,569	32,035	91,297	0	(2,240)	2,245	0	(5)
19	2029	63	60	0	18,585	32,882	42,113	93,580	0	(4,220)	2,282	1,939	0
20	2030	64	61	0	19,482	32,554	43,872	95,919	0	(4,628)	2,319	2,308	0
21	2031	65	62	0	20,503	33,022	44,792	98,317	0	(2,824)	2,358	466	0
22	2032	66	63	0	21,526	33,518	45,731	100,775	0	(2,934)	2,397	538	0
23	2033	67	64	0	22,607	26,475	54,212	103,294	0	(4,570)	2,436	2,134	0
24	2034	68	65	0	23,806	22,835	59,235	105,877	0	(3,098)	2,476	621	0
25	2035	69	66	0	24,993	23,004	60,527	108,524	0	(3,292)	2,517	775	0
26	2036	70	67	0	26,287	11,966	72,983	111,237	0	(6,294)	2,558	3,736	0
27	2037	71	68	0	27,619	10,749	75,650	114,018	0	(6,847)	2,601	4,246	0
28	2038	72	69	0	39,526	0	77,342	116,868	0	(10,110)	3,821	6,289	0
29	2039	73	70	125,000	29,533	11,183	79,074	119,790	0	(9,219)	4,260	4,900	0
30	2040	74	71	0	31,057	10,883	80,845	122,784	0	(7,597)	2,732	4,865	0
Summary											*withdrawal beginning of the following tax year*		
16	2026	60	57	0	15,994	43,844	27,060	86,898	0	(1,116)	2,172	0	(1,056)
31	2041	75	72	0	45,779	0	82,657	125,854	2,581	(11,236)	2,777	5,878	2,581
37	2047	81	78	0	42,443	9,065	94,444	145,952	0	(16,116)	3,063	7,053	0
43	2053	87	84	0	61,292	0	107,968	169,260	0	(18,172)	8,805	9,368	0
48	2058	92	89	0	0	0	120,753	191,502	(70,749)	(842)	4,148	0	(3,304)

Figure 2. An example of projected money coming in (your income) both prior to retirement and at retirement at age fifty-seven. This figure also shows your Income Goal at age fifty-seven, as well as your tax impact prior to and at retirement. Taken together, it shows the net effect of income. Note: these numbers are adjusted for inflation. Created using software by **FPAdvantage** and reproduced with their permission.

We use the information in figure 2 (above) with the Wealth Accumulation information below (figure 3) to help us see the big picture. The information obtained from these two figures will help us determine if we are likely to run out of money before we run out of time.

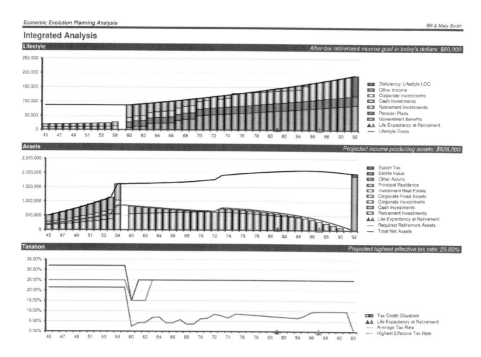

Figure 3. Wealth Accumulation.

Take a moment to think of your entire financial plan as if it's one big treasure map. We've taken the time to identify our goal, our destination: it's the X that marks the spot. Cash flow is taking stock of all the tools you have and all the tools you need in order to get there.

The danger here is that a lot of people just want to stick their head in the sand. It can be pleasant to pick a destination, but it's not quite so fun to figure out exactly how you're going to get there. Taking a long, hard look at your finances, both present and future, can be daunting. Some people just go white in the face when they see their cash flow and realize that there's work to be done.

But what you have to understand is that cash flow is as critical as anything else. No matter who you are, and no matter how much money you have, you'll always have cash coming in and cash going out. If you don't, that means you're dead. I've seen entire companies go under because they ignored their cash flow, airlines especially. Some airlines are always trying to attract customers, thinking that whoever can attract the most is going to get ahead in the game. But it's not that simple. What if fuel prices go up? What if food prices go up? What if they have to replace their aircraft? If you want to see what I mean, check out the long list of failed airlines at www.protectmyholiday.com. Every airline on that list cared solely about attracting customers. They only paid attention to the money coming in. Consequently, they went overboard with their frills.

We had an airline in Canada that was like this. They wanted to take their service to a level beyond what they could actually afford. They didn't look at their cash flow. Nor did they look at what their services were costing them; consequently, they went broke.

On the other hand, some airlines are phenomenally run. Why? They pay attention to their cash flow. They get people where they need to go, consistently, and on time. They don't blow tons of money on amenities or advertising. They concentrate instead on meeting their expenses and their operating costs.

But it's not as simple as tracking how much money you've spent. In fact, I don't *care* what you're spending, *as long as you're saving the right proportion to achieve your goals.* Make a mental note of that fact because it's very important. If you want to go on vacation, go on vacation. If you want to buy a new car, buy a new car. Just make sure your spending isn't going to harm you in the future. If your expenses are paid, and your savings are keeping up with your spending, then you'll probably come out OK. But this ties in with what we talked about before: setting goals and finding out what you really care about. Whether it's retiring at fifty-five, buying a sail boat, whatever—is your current spending getting in the way of your future aspirations? In other words, are you giving up the things you want most for the things you only want right now? Tracking your cash flow is the best way to find out.

A couple more words on cash flow before we move on. There are some very simple things you can do to track your cash flow long before you even meet with a financial planner. How simple? We're talking basic, Junior Achievement-level stuff.

- Balance your chequebook every month. This almost sounds old-fashioned now, considering how many people have stopped using cheques. But even if you do all your spending with cash and debit cards, you still need to "balance your chequebook." How much money are you earning this month? How much do you know you have to spend? How much do you already have in your bank accounts? If you have trouble doing it all by hand, then there are software programs out there that can help you. Quicken is one that I usually recommend.

- Know your expenses. Meet them first, plan ahead for them, and then see what you'll have left. Again, software such as Quicken can help here, too. Whatever money you have left over, spend that. I am not big on budgets because they tend to be very negative. They tell you, "don't do this" and "don't do that." Instead, I advocate figuring out your expenses ahead of time. Here's my recipe for success. From the total income you have after tax, do the following: give some away (10–20 percent); save some (10–20 percent); spend the rest; and do it in that order. You may have to adjust the savings and charity percentages according to your plan, but this basic formula is all you need.*

- Reconcile your chequebook and credit card debt. One of the biggest hurdles people have to overcome, whether they're Canadian or American, is getting out of debt. The main reason is the same old story: people like to stick their head in the sand. They ignore their balances; they toss their statements. It's out of sight, out of mind. Then, when you confront them about it, they basically say, "Gee, I didn't know I had ten credit cards. I thought I had only five."

*You may be wondering why I've put charitable giving in with this formula. I think giving money away to charity is extremely important, and not just for moral reasons. People who have grasped the concept of giving money to charity have moved past the point where greed is a factor. This is important because greed is the downfall of many a financial plan. Greed leads people to make poor financial decisions, especially with their investments. Greedy people always chase after larger and larger returns even if they don't *need* them, and that's no way to invest your money. It almost always leads to trouble.

Enough said about cash flow. Ultimately, it's about tracking how many dollar signs come in and how many go out, and then adjusting the ratio accordingly. It's about your day-to-day life. So long as you don't stick your head in the sand, managing your cash flow will put you on your way to achieving that which you value most.

EDUCATIONAL SAVINGS

This is one of my favourites.

The reason why it's one of my favourites is that education is a big passion of mine. You might not find a section like this in *your* planner's sample, but you can still request that he or she factor it in. The reason why I think it's so important is that, in my life, I've met my share of high school dropouts. Sometimes you can tell how big something is by the space it's supposed to occupy. In this case, I can tell from people who haven't had any education that there's a *big* void that never got filled.

Now, not everybody sees what I see. I've got a lot of people who come to me and say, "I don't see that many high school dropouts." My response is, "Well, what circle do you run in?" If your circle of friends consists solely of old college buddies, wealthy white collars, or university graduates, then yeah, you're not going to see too many dropouts. But there are a lot of them out there.

In some cases, these dropouts have no one to blame but themselves. Some will say, "Well, I wasn't smart enough to go to school." But who's not smart enough to go to school? That's why you *go* to school—to get smart! For others, it might be a cultural thing. If both your mom and dad went to a university, there's a pretty good chance that you will, too. But if neither of your parents sought an education, then your odds go way down. Now, it's true that some dropouts have gone on to become successful in business, like Henry Ford. But it's become more and more difficult to be financially successful in the twenty-first century without an education.

Then, too, it costs a *lot* of money to get an education beyond high school. Take my son, for instance. Right now he's undertaking a college aviation program that we're putting him through. The first year cost is thirty-two thousand dollars. *Thirty-two thousand dollars!* It's a two-year program, which means it'll end up costing sixty-four thousand before he's done. Now you know why there's a shortage of pilots. The same is true of the best universities or technical schools. Why do you think so many cities have a shortage of doctors? Because it costs so much to become one. Without my help, my son would have had to take on student loans to get into college. And if you've ever had student loans, you know that they're pretty easy to get. They're also a lot harder to get rid of.

The point is, so many young people today have neither the money *nor* the influence to go to school. They think, "Mom and Dad didn't do it, and it costs so much money anyway, I might as well get a car and hang out with my friends." Then, when *they* have kids, the same thing happens. It's a vicious cycle. So, if you're a parent or a grandparent, you've got to instill both the value of *and* the opportunity for an education from the time each child comes out of the womb.

This section is for my clients who care about doing what's best for their children or their grandchildren. We can factor education savings into the plan because there are a number of financial incentives out there—government grants and special investment accounts specifically designed for education savings. In some cases, if you contribute your own money up to a certain point, the government will actually subsidize your education savings.

Let's say you don't really care that much for education. I've certainly had a few clients who don't. What happens then? Your daughter drops out of school for all the reasons I listed above, and you just sort of let it happen. "Well," you might say, "she's got a mind of her own. What am I supposed to do?" That's what I see sometimes, parents just throwing their hands in the air, even though that's a major part of parenting. Parenting is all about working with kids, instilling certain values right from the very beginning. But some people say, "Well, there's nothing I can do. My son is on his own."

But here's the thing: he's *not* on his own. Let's say your son turns twenty-five. He didn't get a good education; consequently, he doesn't really have a good job. He has no marketable skills and nothing to put on his résumé. He can't afford to buy a house. Where is he going to live? With you, probably. Or, let's say he gets into debt. Whose door do you think he'll come knocking on? Trying to pinch a few pennies now, at the expense of your children or grandchildren's education, will likely cost you more money down the road.

I didn't realize how big of a problem this is until I started running outside my usual circle. You can divide most of the parents in this world into those who helped their kids out and those who didn't bother to try. Obviously there are exceptions, but, in general, the parent who *can* and *does* invest in his or her own child is the one who gets a good return: a resourceful, self-sustaining kid who won't cost a lot of time and money. Heck, your son or daughter might even take care of *you* one day.

Otherwise, you're going to have a kid who never went to school—or went to school with a bunch of student loans. Then, the first thing she'll learn to do is go bankrupt so that she doesn't have to repay. It's a ridiculous cycle, and ultimately you'll be the one cleaning up her mess. Talk about a drain on your cash flow. That's why education can prove to be a very good investment, for both parents and for their children.

I always say that the best time to plant an oak tree is twenty years ago. The next best time? Right now, with your child. If you weren't saving before, start saving now. A little bit is better than nothing. I want to encourage you to factor your children into the plan. When you talk to your planner, tell him or her that Education Savings should play a part. It might be the best thing you've ever done because you'll make a lot of people grateful: your children, *their* children, and above all…yourself.

KNOW YOU CAN

We just covered some of the most valuable aspects of a good financial plan. Do you want to retire someday? If you structure your plan the way I've just shown you, then you'll know you can. Want to buy that cabin you've always wanted? After calculating your cash flow and making any needed adjustments, you'll know you can. Want to give your children the best chance to succeed in life? Forget about lying in bed at night, worrying. With your financial plan, you'll know you can.

In the next chapter, we'll look at the last sections of your sample financial plan.

FIVE

CREATING A PLAN, PART III

The last sections in our hypothetical plan are as follows:

- Your Family's Security (Insurance)

- Estate Planning

- Investment Strategies (we'll cover this in chapters 8 through 10)

Wait a minute, you say. Insurance? Yes, absolutely insurance. Insurance is a vital part of your plan. Think of insurance as a guarantee for your financial plan to succeed whether you live too long, die too soon, or become disabled. It can keep your plan intact and functioning, even if the worst happens.

Remember: your financial plan is like a pilot's flight plan. Both are supposed to get you from point A to point B. Pilots can't rely solely on navigation to fly their aircraft. They have to know a whole series of emergency procedures in the event of a crisis—how to land in unfamiliar terrain, how to land on water, how to cope when an engine cuts out, you name it. It's these emergency procedures that enable pilots to *stick* to their plan, even when the unexpected comes along.

Insurance has the very same function. Sometimes life throws things at you that even the very best plans can't anticipate. When that happens, do you just cut your losses and bail out? Of course not. You rely on the supports you have in place, on your backup systems, on your fail-safes. It's why car manufacturers put air bags into their cars—so that when you get in an accident, you don't have to think, "Well, bad luck, I'm dead."

Insurance is a fail-safe for your financial plan. It's important that you understand this because insurance is the sort of thing where if your planner has to *sell* you on the concept, you probably won't be buying much of it. But if you understand the true *value* of insurance, it becomes that much easier for your planner to point out the areas in your life that need coverage. It becomes that much easier for you to buy the insurance you need to protect yourself, your family, and your plan—to keep you on the path your plan has set for you.

Think about it: you already rely on insurance to protect your car, should you get in an accident; or your home, if it catches on fire; or your health, if you need to go to the doctor. Doesn't it give you peace of mind to know that you've got a safety net, protecting three of the most important things you own? Now, imagine you can have that same peace of mind if you become disabled or seriously ill. Imagine you can have that peace of mind when it comes to passing on and leaving your loved ones behind.

That's why insurance is such a big part of your financial plan. Sure, you might be able to fly by the seat of your pants and get along without it, but let me tell you this: did you know that most planes can fly with only one engine? It's true. In fact, it would definitely be easier to equip a plane with a single engine. One engine is less to think about than two, and it's also cheaper. But every pilot worth his or her salt is going to fly with two engines because that second engine is *his or her* form of insurance. When I'm flying my plane in the Rockies, for example, I'm always thinking to myself, "One of these engines is going to fail." When I push the throttle forward, I think, "One of these engines is going to fail." When I take off down the runway, I think, "One of these engines is going to fail. Any second now."

Some people might say, "That's negative." No, that's realistic. And it's what *ensures* I'll get from point A to point B. Most pilots would agree that having a second engine provides peace of mind because of the knowledge that the first engine might fail.

Insurance is your second engine.

We'll cover the ins and outs of insurance in chapter 12, but for now, keep this concept in the back of your mind, and don't act skeptical when your planner brings it up. Instead, listen closely. The rule is simple: insure the things you can't afford to lose. It might just save your financial life.

ESTATE PLANNING

Now, let's talk about estate planning.

The most commonly known aspect of estate planning is your will. Most people know what a will is: it's a document that declares how a person's estate should be managed after his or her death and how property should be distributed. But what most people miss is the *point* of creating a will.

A lot of people, when they first come to see me, think that all we're going to do is sit down and fill out a boilerplate will. But this isn't true, and it's not the right attitude to have. A will is *not* an estate plan. It's the document that *executes* your estate plan. As with so many other aspects of financial planning, it's important to understand what it is you're doing and why. True understanding is the difference between a financial planner having to sell you something versus your already appreciating the value of it. The sooner you can truly understand a concept—be it insurance or your will—the sooner you can translate your dreams and concerns into actual numbers.

When most people think of a will, they're really thinking of their *possessions* more than their family. This doesn't necessarily mean they're selfish, just a little naïve. For example, they probably think, "Well, I can't just leave all this stuff of mine lying around after I'm gone, so I better think who it should go to." Or, "I really don't want to see this beautiful house of mine get sold to someone I don't know, so I better give it to my kids."

But this isn't the point. A will isn't about making life easier for your possessions; it's about making life easier for your *family*. For your friends and loved ones. It's more than just thinking, "Well, my daughter Jenny always loved this old diamond ring, so I'll give that to her." That can be part of it, but even more important is, "Jenny's husband is a spendthrift, so I have to make sure there's a provision in my will that ensures he won't spend all of this money after she gets it."

Creating your will is about problem solving. *Solving* problems, not creating them. What we're trying to do here is leave good memories behind—for your family, heirs, and beneficiaries. We don't want to leave issues and problems. But death is always going to cause issues for people, beyond just the emotional kind. Even the money you leave behind is going to be a problem. It doesn't matter how close your family is; if you've got multiple people receiving something from your estate, and you throw money into the middle of the ring among them, there's going to be a problem. *Unless*, of course, you do something about it ahead of time. Every family has disagreements, but that's the whole idea behind your will. It's about keeping your family together.

If you're still not convinced, consider this: What do you think will happen if you *don't* create a will?

Drafting your will is like creating the rules for your own game. A game without rules creates chaos. So, if you don't create the rules, then the government will have to do it. It'll be the government that decides the distribution of your estate and, chances are, it won't be what you wanted.

The government will appoint an administrator, the person in charge of overseeing the distribution of your estate. Now, you might think, *"That's not so bad. They'll probably choose a qualified lawyer or maybe one of my children."* But that's not necessarily true. Anybody—I repeat, *anybody*—can administer a will. Why? Because people can petition for the job, including your cousin Freddie who's addicted to pain killers, drinks too much, and served six months in prison for petty theft.

Not ideal.

So, you really want to create a will. Sure, maybe your cousin Freddie is a long shot to get picked, but why leave it up to chance?

Here's what I do with my clients, and here's what your financial planner should do with you. First, you both should sit down and have a preliminary estate planning meeting. This is where you review the different aspects of estate planning: your will, your enduring power of attorney, your living will, and so on (more on these in a moment). The rules governing each of these are different from province to province or country to country. Although the *concepts* are the same, the rules are different, which is another reason why you should have this meeting.

Next, schedule a meeting with your family. Get everybody together in the same room. Explain to them that you're coordinating with a financial planner. Tell them, "I'm putting together an estate plan, which includes my will. It also takes into consideration taxes, your personalities, charity, the family business, and the list goes on. I'm basically setting the rules for what happens after I die." Then, share with your family some of the specifics, such as

- who will help you write your will;

- who will be the agent overseeing your living will;

- who will have your enduring power of attorney; and

- who will be the executor of your will.

"I'm going to think this all through very carefully," you continue, "but I want you all to know that the reason I'm doing this is that I don't want to create problems for you down the road. So, if you're picked to do something, or if you're *not* picked, it's not because of how I feel about you. It's because my number one priority is not creating problems for anyone. I also want to learn who wants to throw his or her hat in the ring for certain jobs or duties."

That's it. That's what you should say. I promise you, it would make so many people *a lot* happier if this family meeting took place more often. This way, you're starting the process off on the right foot. You're putting everything out into the open. There are no secrets, no intrigue. Just straight-talk. You're finding out which, if any, of your children want to be the executor of your will. (Of course, you'll also need to determine if any of them are *capable* to execute it.) If none of them do, then the next best thing is to find out if you have any trusted friends who are willing and able to do it. If you don't have any, only *then* should you look for a professional trustee to help you. And, as a final note, you can always include in your will and other documents that these representatives will seek out and consider the advice of your financial planner. That way, your planner will be there to hold their hand through the entire process.

Once you go back to meet with your financial planner, it's time to start setting the rules for your own personal game. Your planner will help you answer the following questions:

1. WHO WILL HELP ME WRITE MY WILL?

During my career, I've seen a lot of people try to save a buck when it comes to creating their will. They'll go out and buy "do-it-yourself kits." They're trying to save a buck, and yet their family's welfare is at stake. How can you cut corners when your loved ones' futures are on the line? I don't understand it.

Like I've said time and time again: if it's worth doing, it's worth doing right. That's why I never recommend writing a will yourself. Your will may be a legal document, but it's also contestable. Writing it yourself is just too risky. There's too big a danger that someone will contest something in it, and if you make any mistakes at all, that could really come back to hurt your loved ones down the road.

Now, that's not to say hiring a lawyer is the best route, either—or, at least, hiring *any* lawyer. Just because a lawyer worked on your real estate deal doesn't mean he or she should write your will at the same time. What you ought to do is ask what percentage of a lawyer's practice is devoted to estate law. Anyone who spends 40 percent or more of his or her time on estate law will probably be very good at crafting wills. Your will can still be contested even if a lawyer writes it, so do everything you can to reduce the chances of that happening. Hire a lawyer who specifically practices this kind of law—someone with a great deal of experience. In the end, you don't necessarily need to spend a boatload of money, but you shouldn't look in the bargain basement either. It's less about how much it costs and more about how much time and thought you put into choosing who will help write your will.

2. WHO WILL BE THE AGENT OVERSEEING MY LIVING WILL?

A living will, sometimes called an advance health care directive, is a set of instructions specifying what should happen in the event that you can no longer make decisions for yourself, in case of illness or incapacity. The most commonly known situation featuring a living will is the "pull-the-plug" scenario, when someone is on life support and a family member has to decide whether to continue with care or not.

For this reason, it's typically not a good idea to have close family members, like your children, be the agent of your living will. Pull-the-plug situations—for example, if you were left comatose after a horrendous car accident—are usually just too difficult to cope with. It's not fair to expect your closest loved ones to make that decision. Instead, you want someone who understands your moral beliefs, your ethical beliefs, and your wishes and desires, yet is distant enough to make rational decisions.

I want to stress, too, that your living will extends far beyond "pulling the plug." Life support may not ever be an issue for you. But there *may* come a time when you are not in control of your own faculties, so your family must move you to a long-term care facility. Again, this is where your agent comes in. What long-term care facility will you go to? Who will be allowed to visit you? It's your agent who makes sure these questions are answered the way you would have wanted them to be. These are tough decisions to make, and they can have enormous consequences. I'll give you an example I recently heard about.

To the best of my knowledge, this hasn't happened to any of *my* clients, but what happened was that a family here in Canada had to send their aunt (we'll call her Mabel) to a long-term care facility. Shortly after, Mabel's estranged cousin came to visit. After a nice talk, the cousin led Mabel out of the facility on a little day-trip to her bank. Within minutes, Mabel's bank accounts were empty. The cousin returned Mabel to the facility and then disappeared into the night.

So, your living will is about more than just when to pull the plug; it's about who can have access to you when you're at a disadvantage. With a living will, you can decide who can see you and who can't, or who needs a chaperone, and it's your agent who'll make sure your wishes are carried out. This is why estate planning is so important, and why it's critical to choose people you can trust. I promise you, most lawyers aren't going to help you decide these things. They're not going to go through the nitty-gritty with you. That's why you need a planner and an agent who are both familiar with you and with the nasty things that sometimes happen. You need someone who will prevent those nasty things from happening to you because, again, estate planning is all about keeping your family together. How can that happen if you're exposing yourself to criminals or mistakes or accidents?

Here's another important consideration. If you don't have a living will, anyone can apply to become your trustee or guardian. Sometimes the results are disastrous. For instance, I met a woman once, who we'll call Alice. Alice was a very prominent citizen from Edmonton. When we met, she'd been married to her husband John for over twenty years. But John had a wife from a prior marriage. The children from his previous marriage lived in a different city in Alberta, and they weren't very close. The main reason was that they didn't like Alice.

Alice came to me because John had just suffered a stroke, rendering him incapacitated. Now, like I said, Alice was a very prominent citizen, and her husband was even more so. But he had no will. He had no enduring power of attorney. No living will. He just never saw fit to get that stuff done. So, now, Alice was tasked with taking care of him because the stroke had basically left him a vegetable. But while the responsibility to take care of him was hers, the legal right fell to his estranged children.

After John's stroke, Alice stayed by his side for months and months. While she was doing that, his estranged children were applying to become his trustee and guardian. Since there was no living will or enduring power of attorney, pretty much anybody, even his next door neighbour, could apply. Of course, it might seem a little unusual to choose John's neighbour for the job, but his children? To the court, it would seem perfectly reasonable. How could the court know they were estranged? How could the court know John's children had no regard for their stepmother, who was at that very moment trying to nurse her husband back to health? They couldn't know. The only way to tell them was to create a living will and enduring power of attorney.

When Alice learned about this, she went into a complete panic because all John's children wanted to do was come in and run the companies he owned. They didn't care about her *or* him. That's a terrible situation to get into. In the end, the whole thing devolved into a protracted legal battle, but it could have been averted if John had taken the time to plan ahead.

So, that's your living will. It's crucial you create one, and it's equally crucial to name an agent you trust. Again, your children might not be the best choice. Even if you trust them, it can be a very, very challenging job. Are your children prepared to do it indefinitely? Do they have the time? Can they handle it emotionally? Is there going to be unrest amongst the other family members because they're doing it? If you can't answer all those questions to your satisfaction, consider naming someone else. And, as always, consult with your planner before making the choice.

3. WHO WILL HAVE MY ENDURING POWER OF ATTORNEY?

The term "power of attorney" basically means "someone appointed to act on another's behalf." Under normal circumstances, we usually refer to this as "general power of attorney." *Enduring* power of attorney is a bit different. From a functional standpoint, your general power of attorney and your enduring power of attorney can do the same things. But general power of attorney is null and void if you become mentally incapacitated. When that happens, your enduring power of attorney takes over. Whoever you name to the job is the one who will take care of your finances if you're ever unable to. Typically, your enduring power of attorney has to report to the public trustee, as well as to the executor of your estate. At least with this job there's some form of oversight.

Again, it's typical to see people appoint their favourite son or daughter, or the one whom they feel is the best with money. What people don't appreciate is that their children have full-time jobs or families of their own, so they may not be the best choice to take care of your estate. Even if your children have the capability, they might not have the time. They may not even have the desire to do it. Again, always find out these things ahead of time. As we discussed, give your children and friends the *option* to do it. But if they're not the best choice or don't want to do it, then you can consider a financial expert, like a professional trustee. (Your planner can't do it because there might be a conflict of interest.)

A professional trustee can potentially be a good choice because

- he or she is emotionally disinterested;

- it reduces the possibility of jealousy in the family; and

- he or she may have skills and knowledge no one else in your family is likely to have.

You don't *have* to hire a professional. You can use one of your kids if he or she has the time, the capability, and the desire, but make sure you choose only *one* child. Otherwise, you'll have conflict. If one of your kids is the obvious choice, then great. If not, consider your other options, such as a friend or professional trustee (in that order) as explained above. Also, be wary of letting your accountant or lawyer have your enduring power of attorney because their fees might eat into your estate. Ultimately, we don't want you to end up like John and Alice. Whoever you choose, make sure you give it a *lot* of thought first.

One final point on your enduring power of attorney. When you work with your planner, make sure the document that names your trustee *specifically* states that the trustee "is obligated to consult with your financial planner." If the trustee is your child, then the child "should consult if practical." This should be written right into the document. It will help ensure that your trustee makes decisions in accordance with your financial plan.

Another concept to be aware of is a *springing* power of attorney. "Springing" means that this power of attorney doesn't spring into action until two medical professionals determine whether or not you are incapable of handling your money. It's their job to decide whether your springing power of attorney needs to take over or not.

Stick with me here—all these terms might seem incomprehensible at first, but they'll make sense once you become familiar with them. If your enduring power of attorney is *immediate*, meaning that it takes effect immediately, you don't need any medical practitioners to sign off on it. But your *springing* power of attorney *could* require those two practitioners.

One technique is that we can choose to name a person as your immediate representative, as well as a more restricted alternate, all on the same document. The alternate would be required to have two practitioners determine that you are incapable of handling your own affairs before he or she could do anything.

It's always a good idea to name someone as an alternate representative on your power of attorney, just in case the first person you pick isn't capable of doing it when the time comes (maybe they are incapacitated, too). But maybe it's impossible to find an alternate whom you trust as much as the person you named on your immediate enduring power of attorney. For example, let's say you name your spouse on your immediate enduring power of attorney. But you need an alternate, and while you believe the person you name can do the job, you might not be *quite* as confident in that person as you are in your spouse. So, you name your spouse on your immediate power of attorney, meaning he or she can act on your behalf immediately should the need ever arise. This could be advantageous because if you're traveling on business while trying to sell your house, you'd need signatures to complete the sale. If your spouse is on your immediate power of attorney, he or she can sign while you're away. Meanwhile, your alternate can be restricted to require two medical professionals to determine whether or not you're capable of handling your affairs before any action is taken. That way, you have the safeguards in place to ascertain whether your alternate *truly* needs to take over because two medical professionals have to sign off on it.

By the way, I'm not necessarily advising that you name your spouse on your immediate enduring power of attorney. I've heard of people who went to work in the morning, only to come home to find their spouse had gone to the bank and cleaned them out. Could that happen to you? I have no idea. The point is, give this process a *lot* of thought before making a decision.

In the end, it'll be your lawyer's job to review your situation and make the appropriate suggestions—with input from your planner—because your planner will have the most intimate knowledge of you and your financial situation. Just remember: you have to name a representative on your enduring power of attorney to protect yourself if you're ever incapacitated. Whoever you name should be competent...*and* trustworthy.

4. WHO WILL BE THE EXECUTOR OF MY WILL?

Many of the topics we covered above also apply to your will. Your main decision is choosing your executor. Your executor is the person who ensures that the provisions of your will get carried out. Again, one of the biggest mistakes I see is people naming their children without thinking about it. That's a problem because the decision requires a *lot* of thought. If you name just one child, there's a good chance the others will take offense. Or, they may not trust the child you named to execute the will properly. Some parents overcompensate and name *all* their children. But what if each child lives in a different province? What if they don't get along? What if they don't communicate well with each other?

Besides, one child will always be the dominant one, but he or she will be hampered by the fact that everything has to be decided in committee. It rarely creates anything but problems—and remember, your will is supposed to *solve* problems, not create them.

The best thing to do is have another family meeting, preferably in your planner's office. Sit everyone down and say, "Here are the three documents we're drafting. Here is who'll be running my living will, and it's not going to be any of you because I don't feel any of you should have to make these decisions. I don't want to put you in the place where you have to decide whether to pull the plug on me.

"I also have my enduring power of attorney. I'm going to choose Uncle Bill to do that because he'll be impartial, he has the time, and he has the experience to do it. And for my will, I'm going to choose Uncle Bill as well. My friend Bob will be the alternate on both documents because he's capable, I trust him, and it will take all the pressure off you kids."

Now, maybe you think I'm making a mountain out of a molehill here. After all, these are your *kids* I'm talking about. But I've based everything in this book on my *personal experience* as a financial professional. I see these problems all the time, and the whole point of this book is so you can learn from other people's mistakes. It's cheaper for you that way. But if you really want to choose your kids, if you feel like it makes the most sense, ask your children who *they* think should be your executor. Maybe one of them will throw his or her hat in the ring. If your other kids are fine with that—*truly* fine, without a hint of hesitation—then great. Or, maybe no one will throw his or her hat in. Maybe you've got three kids, and two come flat out and say they won't do it. If that's the case, don't lay it on the third one. If the third one didn't even volunteer, he or she is definitely not the right candidate. It's too big a job to lay on anyone who doesn't want to do it. That's when you really need to start thinking of someone else. Whatever you do, don't select someone without his or her permission.

The point is, *get your family involved.* You have to have this conversation with them because it's not the kind of talk you can have with your lawyer. Your lawyer will just say, "Well, who do you want to name as executor?" Your lawyer's just there to put a name to paper. You probably won't get advice or recommendations unless you're paying him or her big bucks; your lawyer's job is just to file you in and file you out. So, have the conversation with your financial planner, have it with your family, and then you can finally get down to the task of completing your will.

One final story, just to prove my point. I could write a book full of cases like this, but one is enough.

I worked with a family once whom we'll call the Colemans. Mother and Father Coleman had six children altogether. They named the oldest as the executor of their estate. After they died, their family was completely driven in half. *Everything* the oldest daughter tried to do was challenged. It wasn't a large estate, only $300,000 or so, but after a while it dwindled down to almost nothing. Why? Because the children took everything to court. They fought about this; they fought about that. At one point, they fought over whether the daughter should be paid a fee for her services as an executor, when she didn't even *want* to be paid a fee! But somehow the issue came up, and one faction in the family wouldn't stand for it. Their sister could *not* be paid a fee. Their attitude backfired, however, because finally the judge banged his metaphorical gavel and said, "No, she is going to be paid for her services. End of story." And that was that. They couldn't fight it anymore.

When the battle was done, they looked around and surveyed the damage. It looked just like the aftermath of every battle: carnage. Their estate was devastated, their relationships with each other ruined—and all because Mommy Coleman and Daddy Coleman didn't take the time to get their wills done *right*. They didn't have their family meetings. The result was a will that *created* problems instead of *solving* them.

The moral of the story? Figure out what you want. Figure out what your family wants. Think about each question above, and think about them carefully. Be thorough. If there's *anything* in your life that could be misunderstood or could cause a dispute, then spell it out in your will.

That way, it won't be just your possessions you leave behind; it'll be a lifetime of happy memories.

KNOW YOU CAN

One of the greatest benefits of having a financial plan is the peace of mind it provides. Nowhere is that more apparent than when it comes to your estate. With a financial plan in place, you can feel certain both you and your family will always be taken care of. A good financial plan means protection against being taken advantage of. It means you will *always* control your finances, even if you become ill or infirm. You might not be able to dictate what happens to you in life, but with a financial plan, you can dictate how you'll respond.

Another benefit is that your financial plan will solve problems before they even happen. Want to make life easier on your children after you're gone? Want to maintain harmony in your home? Want to protect yourself from the risks that come with long-term care?

With a financial plan, you'll know you can.

SIX

HOW TO ENSURE YOU HAVE A GOOD PLAN

In chapter 2, I mentioned that if something's worth doing, it's worth doing right. To do something right, you need a plan.

But how do you know if your *plan* is right? After all, there are plans, and there are *plans*. Some plans may be good in theory but impossible in practice. Some might be just boilerplate plans that aren't specific to you. Some plans might not take certain things into account. And some plans aren't really plans at all.

What I hope is that, after finishing the previous chapter, you closed the book, looked in the mirror, and said to yourself, "I need a plan." If you haven't done that yet, go ahead and do it now. Say it to your spouse. Say it out loud. But say it. It's time to get started.

Now you've arrived at one of the most important parts of the process: the part where you've come to a realization, made a decision, and are wondering what to do next. The people who never get past this stage are the ones who just keep wondering and wondering. Ultimately, that wondering just becomes a new form of procrastination. So, in this chapter, we're going to take the wonder off the table and outline what you need to do next, and how you should go about doing it.

First, consider the following:

1. CAN I CREATE A PLAN ON MY OWN, OR DO I NEED HELP?

These days, we're all looking to save a buck. That thrifty attitude has led many of us to becoming the "do-it-yourself" type of person. We fix our own cars, remodel our own houses, prepare our own taxes, and so on.

The quandary here is that, these days, it's becoming harder and harder to do things yourself. Why? Think of all the questions that need to be answered:

- Do I have the desire to do it myself?

- Do I have the resources/money to do it myself?

- Do I have the knowledge to do it myself?

- Do I have the support to do it myself?

- Do I have the time to do it myself?

Many people might have the resources and the smarts to do something, but they might not have the desire. A lack of desire is death to a good financial plan. It will show in every aspect. Others might have the skills but not the resources, or they have the resources but not the time.

On the other hand, maybe you *don't* have the skills. There's probably a pretty good chance that you don't do your own dental work. You certainly wouldn't operate on yourself. You might have a clue about dentistry, but you don't do your family's dental work because you don't practice. That's not what you do.

Even something as fundamental as fixing your own car is becoming more difficult. Sure, we all admire the person who can throw on a pair of overalls, pop the hood, and fix the problem, but these days, cars are becoming so complicated that you need special tools and devices to even tell what the problem is. It's more like working with a computer than with an automobile. Financial planning is much the same way. There's so much to know and so much to do that, unless you have special training and experience, it's absurd to expect an average person to create his or her own plan.

If the answer to any of these questions is *no,* then trying to create your own plan just isn't a good idea. In the end, not only will you save time and money by getting help, but you'll also do it *right.*

2. SO, HOW DO I GET HELP?

The answer to this is simple: you hire a financial planner. But what exactly is a financial planner?

The easy answer is that you're looking for anyone with the letters **CFP** attached to the end of his or her name. CFP, which stands for Certified Financial Planner, is a *global* designation. It's good in Canada; it's good in the United States; and it's good in most other parts of the world. To earn the designation, one has to meet a few requirements: a certain amount of education, a certain amount of work experience, a passing score on some examinations, and so on. There are other designations you can find, too. In Canada, for example, you have Registered Financial Planners, Chartered Financial Planners (now referred to as Certified Financial Planners), and the like. In many cases, these different titles can overlap. A planner can hold more than one designation, but for our purposes, let's stick with CFP.

Anyone with CFP after his or her name is a legitimate financial planner. That's definitely a good place to start. Let it be your minimum requirement when choosing who you want to work with. Even with that criterion, though, your search is still going to be pretty broad. There are many, many people who can boast the CFP title. What, then, are you really looking for?

The problem with basing your selection solely on three letters is that a designation only indicates a person's education. It doesn't tell you his or her practice. It doesn't reveal his or her *specialty.* Think of it like this: every doctor in the United States and Canada has an MD attached to his or her name. The letters "MD" indicate that they've been to medical school, that they're trained and educated and are fully qualified to be doctors. Still, there are different *types* of doctors, aren't there? The most basic one is a general practitioner—the one you go to when you've got a sore throat. But a general practitioner is not an oncologist. General practitioners know a lot about cancer, of course, and they'll have *studied* a lot about cancer, but it's not their specialty. It's not their practice. So, if you've got cancer, you need to see an oncologist, not a general practitioner. Yet, both the oncologist and the general practitioner will have the same basic designation: MD.

The same is true of financial professionals. You don't have to solely be a financial planner in order to have the CFP designation. Accountants can have it. So can stockbrokers. They'll have studied financial planning, but that doesn't mean they *practice* it. In most cases, a professional will tell you if what you're looking for is beyond the scope of his or her job—but not always. Some people have big egos. Some people like to play God. Some people just want your money.

Let's frame it like this: imagine it's April, and you're getting your taxes done. Your sister refers you to someone she knows. You set an appointment and go to his office. You notice that it says "Tax Planner" on his desk. Come to think of it, his door said Tax Planner, too, as did his company letterhead. When you question him about it, you find that all he does is prepare tax returns.

Wait a minute. Preparing a return is *not* a plan. How could it be? The definition of "plan" is "a scheme or method of acting, doing, proceeding, making; developed in advance." The key words there are *"in advance."* But a tax return is basically a report of *what has already happened*. So, preparing tax returns isn't planning; it's record-keeping.

Real planning doesn't involve reporting what you've already done. It's *deciding in advance what you want to do*. Tax planning is investigating and selecting the various means of legally reducing your taxes *in the future*. That's the critical distinction. Calling yourself a tax planner doesn't automatically make it so. Actually *planning* your future taxes is what makes it so.

The same is true for financial planning, and *that's* what you need to look for. You're looking for people who actually practice the art of planning finances.

What does "planning finances" actually mean? We've already defined *planning* as making decisions *for the future*. All that's left is to look at the word "finances."

Put in a personal context, the word "finances" refers to every aspect of your life that has to do with money. Your expenses relate to finances. So do your savings. Your needs *and* your wants. Your retirement. Your debt. Your investments, insurance, taxes, retirement, social security, real estate—all of it. So, planning your finances means that you've decided *in advance*:

- How to maintain your expenses so that you can pay for both your needs and your wants

- How to pay down your debt

- How much taxes you are going to pay

- What to invest in and what the profits from those investments will be used for

- What insurance you need

- How to pay for retirement

- How your assets will be handled after you die

A financial planner is both educated *and* practiced at handling all of these things. That's why you can't rely just on a set of credentials. That's why you can't just rely on a sign on the door.

The frustrating thing for me personally is there are many professionals who *think* of themselves as financial planners who really aren't. For instance, someone who calls herself a "financial advisor" may in fact do bona fide financial planning, or she may not. Maybe she just recommends investments. If that's the case, she's not a planner; she's an investment advisor.

Or, maybe you meet with an accountant who calls himself a financial planner. But calling himself one doesn't make it so. I've actually had people come to me and show me the "plan" that some accountant came up with, and it usually consists of a few sheets of paper. Each sheet will have some generic, nonspecific advice written on it, consisting of gems like "Ensure you will have enough money to meet your expenses when you retire." I'm telling you, it reads like a fortune cookie!

Or, maybe there's a will attached. When it was written, the lawyer probably just sat down with him and asked, "Where do you want everything?"

"I want everything to go to my children."

"Great," the lawyer says. He writes that down and puts it in the will. But what he *didn't* do was ask if those children are young children or adult children, if any of them have issues, or if there are any individual trusts for them already existing. He never once went into the details.

If you want to boil it down to one thing, then the difference between a real financial planner and someone who *calls* himself one is this: a real financial planner knows the questions to ask. There are people out there who give professional planners a bad name, but if your planner is asking questions about *you*, if he or she genuinely wants to know the answers and sincerely cares about *you*, then chances are that your planner is a good one. Furthermore, your planner should then work with your lawyer and accountant to coordinate your plan as a team.

Later in the chapter, we'll explore those questions.

3. WHAT IF I CAN'T FIND A GOOD PLANNER? SHOULD I DO IT MYSELF AFTER ALL?

No, no, and *no*. Remember, a good planner knows what questions to ask you. Do *you* know what questions to ask yourself? You probably don't. You'll know a lot of them after reading this book, but there will be some I didn't cover, questions that only someone who has sat down and met with you could know to ask.

When you do it yourself, you also run the risk of overlooking important items. It's the difference between a one-crew airplane and a two-crew airplane. If you were flying solo, you would still have a checklist to go through before you take off. Good pilots know to read the checklist out loud, as if they were talking to someone. While this helps, there's still no one there to make sure you didn't miss anything. With a two-crew plane, though, you have the checks and balances you need to make sure nothing is missed. You have a co-pilot to go through the checklist with you to ensure everything is done right.

Your financial planner is your co-pilot.

Here's the way it works. A good planner will always ask the right questions. Once your planner has the answers to those questions, he or she will be able to provide you with an incredible plan. It'll have insights into who *you* are, what *you* want, what *you* care about, and what you're willing to do for it. There's a good chance you'll even learn some things about yourself that you never realized before. Most of us simply aren't going to ask ourselves those questions. Oftentimes, we think we already know the answers to those questions, but we haven't even heard the questions yet!

But for the sake of conversation, let's pretend for a minute you *do* know what questions to ask. That's wonderful, but will you be able to come up with the right answers? Some questions require you to look outside yourself rather than within. I'm talking about technical questions, legal questions, logistical questions. Sure, you can always Google something, but who's providing the response? Is it a credible source? A good planner relies on *several* sources and has probably tested them over many years to make sure they're credible. If a source is *not* credible, he or she has something to test it against. What do you have to test your source against?

Finally, let's imagine that you *do* know which questions to ask, and you *can* trust whatever sources you find. You'll still have a hard time coming up with a real plan. Why? Because the information you find *won't be specific to you.* It'll be generalized. Indiscriminate. General information might apply to the majority, but it very well might not apply to you. Think of it this way: maybe you're having some health problems, some symptoms that you can't explain. So, you fire up Google and start browsing. You'll probably find some good sites, like WebMD and the Mayo Clinic site. But you'd have to be pretty foolish to diagnose yourself based on what you read there. You'd have to be even more foolish to decide what medicine to take or what foods to eat. What you find will be general information that *won't* take into account aspects that are unique to you. Maybe you're allergic to the type of foods that general information recommends you take. Maybe the recommendations would interfere with other conditions you have. The point is, Google can't replace your doctor, just as it can't replace a good financial planner. Google can search, but it can't listen. Nor can it think.

As to whether you can *find* a good planner or not, take it from me: you can. It's the twenty-first century. Just because you don't see a planner in your yellow pages doesn't mean he or she isn't out there. Ask your friends, your family, or your neighbours. Ask the people in your place of worship if any of them know of a good planner. Then, check with your employer or your spouse's employer. Many large companies will provide you access to a planner they're already working with. For example, at HSI, we work with employers to provide their employees with educational sessions where we introduce them to financial planning. Many employers realize that a financially successful individual makes a great employee and brings less baggage to the workplace. It's worth your time to ask around.

If that's a dead end, take to the Internet. Google can't create a plan for you, but it can find someone who can. Even if there's no one in your area, many planners will come to you. If that doesn't work, find someone who will do it remotely. There are plenty of online planners you can work with. Check to make sure they have references and that they're rated well. But that's research you should do anyway.

Regardless of the source, good planners are out there. Find them.

Once you've found help, the fun begins.

It's not possible for me to take you from A to Z through the whole process, and it's beyond the scope of this book because different planners will have their own way of doing things. But there are some things every planner should do, things that will tell you if your planner is good or not and, by extension, if your *plan* is good.

1. YOUR PLANNER SHOULD MAKE YOU FEEL COMFORTABLE

This is a must. In fact, it should make or break any potential relationship you form with your planner. If you're not comfortable with your planner, then you won't feel comfortable with your plan. Why? Because you won't have told the planner everything she needs to know. Understand, it's not an *easy* thing to talk about your money. No one is saying it is. I've met people who are more comfortable talking about sex than they are about money. Whether it's because you don't really trust the person you're talking to, or because you're embarrassed, going into detail about your finances can be a painfully revealing process. Part of the planner's job is to take the pain *out* of that process. If she doesn't, chances are you won't tell her everything she needs to know. If you hold things back, your plan won't represent you entirely. It'll represent you partially. It'll represent only the things you told your planner about.

It's important that you're comfortable. It's like going in for a checkup and not feeling good about your doctor. Would you tell someone you're not comfortable with intimate details about your body? Of course not. So, you aren't doing yourself any favours by visiting a doctor you don't like. You're not doing the *doctor* any favours either, since without *all* the information, he can't do his job to the best of his ability. It's the same thing with planners.

If at some point during this process you look across the desk at your planner and think, "I just don't feel good about being here" or "Something about the guy just *bugs* me," then don't hesitate. Stand up, shake his hand, explain that it's not going to work out, and then walk away. Simple as that. Don't worry about the planner's feelings. Worry about *yours*. You'll actually be doing him a favour. Planners don't like working with people they don't get along with any more than you do. After all, the planner is picking *you* just as much as you are picking him.

Always ask yourself, "Am I comfortable? Am I willing to tell my planner everything?" If not, walk away. If you are, keep reading.

2. YOUR PLANNER SHOULD SPEND TIME WITH YOU

Unfortunately, you can't rely on comfort alone to gauge your planner's expertise. You can't choose a planner just because he or she is a nice person. I know lots of nice people who are not very good at what they do. I often say that I'm always ready to be *friends* with nice people, but I'm not always ready to do *business* with them.

Similar to that is the concept of trust. It's obviously critical that you trust your planner, but again, it can't be the sole factor. Besides, we apply different rules of trust for different people. It might take us a long time to trust someone we meet on the street, but when you meet your new brother-in-law for the first time? Chances are, trust is going to come a lot faster. But should it? If you're choosing between your brother-in-law and the guy on the street when it comes to managing your money, then the answer is no. Trust shouldn't come faster. There's really no difference between the two. You don't *know* either person. You might be comfortable with your brother-in-law, but you shouldn't trust him based solely on that. He's as liable to be incompetent as anybody else. In general, be careful of family and friends when choosing your financial planner. Can you fire *them* if something goes wrong?

What's more, trust should be earned, not given. How does a planner earn your trust? Ask yourself these questions, and see if the answers satisfy you:

- How much time did my planner spend with me?

- What kinds of questions did he or she ask me?

- Did he or she answer all *my* questions?

During my career, I've had *many* people come through my door after previously working with someone else. Usually they're frustrated, but they're not sure *why* they're frustrated. First, I ask them, "How much time did your planner spend with you?" Most people say, "Well, we just kind of got rushed through the whole process." As soon as they say that, they know. That was a big red flag, and they missed it. If you feel rushed through the process, your plan probably isn't going to be very good. Maybe it won't really be a plan at all. Comb through the history books if you don't believe me. How many great plans were rush jobs?

Look at those three questions again. They're great questions because each one leads into the next one. The more time your planner spends with you, the more likely you'll be asked the *right* kinds of questions. A rushed planner, for example, would probably only ask you the following:

- How much money do you have/earn?

- When do you want to retire?

- Where do you want all your money to go after you're dead?

Then, the planner would plug a few numbers into an impressive-looking computer program and print out an incomprehensible spreadsheet. If you took the time to actually decipher it, you'd probably realize that all it says is what you already know—the things *you* told the planner. At this point, you'd better be fuming because you certainly didn't intend on paying the planner for *data entry*. You wanted a *plan*.

Planners who take their time with you will still ask those questions, but they're also going to have all kinds of follow-up questions. How much money do you earn at your job? How much do you have invested? How much do you have in savings? How much insurance do you have, and what kinds? What are your five top personal goals, and in what order would you rank them? Are you willing to work longer to ensure you'll have the money to reach those goals, or is it a requirement that you retire by age sixty-five? What are your real estate holdings? How many children do you have? How many grandchildren? What are their personalities? What do they want and what do they *need*? How much do you value this versus how much you value that?

And so on. When that's done, sure, they'll stick the answers you give them into some kind of document or spreadsheet, but they'll *explain* it to you. They'll go over every form, point by point, and they'll take their time. They'll explain why your answers are important. They'll explain what your answers require. And they'll answer *your* questions—not somebody else's questions and not a list they dug up labeled "Frequently Asked Questions (FAQ)." *Your* questions.

If you're treated like that, then you can feel a lot more confident that you have a good planner, and thus a good plan. Good planners leave no stones unturned. They take the time to make sure you understand how it works (which makes sense, considering the plan is supposed to be *for you*, and you're the one who will have to execute it). Too many people in the financial services industry just want to say, "Next, next, who's next? Take a number, sit down, wait your turn, and then please make way for the next person." Everybody gets into the same investment program. There's no strategy. There's no conversation about problem-solving if you *have* a problem. But what if you lose your job? What if you get sick? What's the answer? Shouldn't planners *know* this stuff?

Of course they should. So, you'd better have that conversation because *that's* how you'll know if you have a good plan.

3. YOUR PLANNER SHOULD WRITE DOWN YOUR PLAN

Simple, but essential. If your plan isn't written down, if it's not in a form that you can see and hold, that's a problem. You'd have to memorize it. But trying to memorize your plan would be a disaster. You'd forget things or change things in your mind. Instead of being a tangible roadmap you can always refer to, it will be just a wisp of smoke. Insubstantial. Impossible to maintain.

Your plan doesn't necessarily have to be printed on paper; uploading it to your computer works just fine, as long as it's written down. It's the only way you'll be able to actually follow it.

4. YOUR PLANNER SHOULD FIND OUT WHAT'S IMPORTANT TO YOU

This one is critical.

I said above that your planner knows the right questions to ask, and I even gave a few examples. But these were financial, numbers-oriented questions. Important, but insufficient. You can ask numbers-oriented questions until the cows come home, but you still won't have a real plan.

Think of it like this. You're building a house. You hire someone to help you design it, and you really get into the details—the size of this room, the size of that one, the layout, the dimensions, the materials. But is that all you have to decide? Of course not. You have to tell the designer what you *want*. How will the lighting work? When will the sun come in through this window, and when will it come through that one? How do you want your rooms painted? How do you want them decorated afterwards? Will your possessions fit in the room after the house is built? If you have kids, are there any factors in the design that could cause them to get hurt? The person who's working with you to build the house should be spending the time to find out what you really care about, so that when you're done, you have more than just a house. You have a home.

A good planner will ask you what you care about. What are your attitudes? What are your values? What are the things that *have* to happen for you to be happy? What are the things you'd only *like* to have in order to be happy?

If your planner doesn't ask those things, your plan will reflect that. It'll be just a bunch of numbers. Here's an example: say you sit down with a planner, and you show him how much money you have, how much debt, and so on. You ask him, "How much money do I need to be able to retire?" He crunches the numbers and hands you a printout with the total on it. You say, "Great!" and head home, the figure he gave you floating around in your head.

At first, it seems like a magic number, and you work towards it. When you finally get there, you think, *"Now I can retire."* Only, when you retire, you realize that maybe the number wasn't all it was cracked up to be. Sure, you've retired, but all that number got you was the means to settle your debts and pick out a family plot or go to the doctor once in a while. The number enabled you to retire, but it didn't allow you to *do* anything after you retired. It only factored in what you needed to *live*...not what you needed to live *happily*. So, you didn't really have a plan. I often say, "If you don't have a plan, you'll probably become part of someone else's...and you probably won't like it."

Or maybe your planner took into account a comment you made when you said you'd love to have a motor home so you could travel the country. Well, great. You buy your motor home. Only now you realize that your money's gone, so you can't do all the other things you planned to do, like contribute to different charities and causes or help out your old high school or set money aside so your grandkids can go to college. You might feel pretty awful when you're visiting Banff, knowing you *could* have done all these other wonderful things—the things you always *promised* yourself you'd do as soon as you got the chance. But your "plan" factored in only the motor home. It didn't have anything in there about how much you'd love to help women with breast cancer. It didn't take into account how much you love your grandkids. It didn't have anything in there about how much you'd love to take up stargazing or add another room to your house. For that matter, it didn't even take into account whether you can afford enough gas to run the motor home. It didn't have those things because your planner didn't know to put them in. *Because he didn't ask.*

A lot of these questions should be asked in your initial planning meeting. I personally make it a point to find out these things right at the onset. From my perspective, it helps me do two things:

- Figure out if I can work with this person

- Figure out the style of plan I'll need to help them create it, and whether it's realistic

Remember what I said earlier about feeling comfortable with your planner? It goes both ways. Often if you're not feeling comfortable with your planner, then your planner probably isn't feeling comfortable with you. This can happen if the values of the client and planner are diametrically opposed. For example, I've had people come in for their first planning meeting with me, and right from the beginning, I knew things were going to be difficult. They may say they care more about their dogs than they do their kids. I can't tell them what they should or should not feel, but in my opinion, caring more about your dog than your kids is not a good thing. It's not easy for me to work with people like that, and it probably won't be easy for them to work with me.

Sometimes I'll have new clients say to me, "My last guy didn't ask me what I care about." I'll ask them, "What kind of questions *did* he ask you?" Their answer, more often than not, is "How much money do you have to invest? Where do you want to invest it?" That's what their last guy asked them. The worst is, "How much money do you need for retirement?" Then they'll say, "I don't know. That's why I came to you." So, then, their last guy will do what I said above and just hand them a printout with a number on it.

Well, what was that number based on? When my clients come to me, I'll give them a number, too, but it'll be *based* on something. Sometimes that number will even change if the factors it's based on have changed. For example, if you came to me at thirty years old, gave me your income and expenses, and told me your wants, dreams, and wishes, we could sit down and determine what you'd need for retirement. But that number might be different at age forty-five or age sixty. Your income and expenses probably aren't going to be the same, but just as important, your dreams and wishes probably won't be the same either. The wants of a thirty-year-old are usually different from the wants of a sixty-year-old. Your values, your attitudes, and your outlook on life might be very different as well. So, with some clients, their number might change a dozen times. *That's* why it's so important to find out what you care about—so we can actually base the plan on something.

Another reason these questions help is that they'll aid your planner in determining the type of person you are. Are you a spendthrift? Frugal? Just a common-sense type of person? That'll determine in large part how much your income and expense recommendations are adjusted. That's why boilerplate plans just don't work. A plan for a frugal person would be disastrous for a spendthrift. They're going to want and need different things. Good planners will recommend the spendthrift have a lot higher income and a lot more set aside than they will the frugal person.

First, take some time *now* to ask yourself these questions:

- What's important to me?

- What do I care about?

- *Who* do I care about?

- What do I want to accomplish in this world?

- What do I want to leave behind?

Answering these now will make it easier to work with your planner later. Moreover, it'll prevent you from any nasty surprises down the road. I'll give you an example.

A few years ago, a husband and wife came to see me. Let's call them Ed and Linda. We went through the whole planning process with them: income, expenses, investments, you name it. Everything was going fine until we started talking about estate planning—more specifically, their wills.

During the whole meeting, Linda was really enthusiastic, whereas Ed was acting increasingly distant. Every time I tried to learn more about *him*, tried to find out what made him tick, he withdrew. By the time we got to the wills, you could feel the tension in the room. You could cut it with a knife, it was so thick. I had to drag everything out of him. If I talked to Linda, then he acted like he wasn't even there. He just sat in his chair, not saying anything. It was really, really odd.

I didn't know at the time what his problem was. But a few weeks later, I phoned Linda. I asked her if she knew what was wrong with her husband. From the other end, I heard the tears begin to flow. I got a sick feeling in my stomach because I knew what was coming.

Apparently, it took this planning process for Ed to realize what he really valued in his life. It wasn't Linda. He realized that he did not want to be with her anymore. He didn't love her. She was *not* the most important thing in his life, and so he couldn't base his decisions around a lie. This is what my questions uncovered, for him and for her. It even led to his admitting that he had once had an affair.

Granted, this is a pretty extreme case. Usually, planning is an *affirming* process, not a negative one. But think if I hadn't asked those questions. Imagine if I hadn't tried to dig deeper. Sure, we could have put their plan together. We could have made up their wills. But what would have been the point? It wouldn't have made Ed happy, and he probably wouldn't have followed the plan anyway because the plan wouldn't have been for him. It wouldn't have reflected who he *truly* was and what he *truly* wanted.

The planning process didn't create Ed and Linda's problems, but it did bring them to light. Once they took a long look at their situation, they got honest with each other. The moral of the story is to figure out who you are and what you want *now,* for yourself and your family. If your planner does the same, you can feel pretty sure that your plan is based off what *really* matters: you.

That's how you'll know if you have a good planner. That's how you'll know if you have a good plan.

KNOW YOU CAN

Choosing a good financial planner can seem daunting, but it's by no means difficult or impossible. All it requires is some thoroughness on your part. If you take your time in choosing a planner and if you make sure your planner meets all the criteria outlined above, then you'll know you've chosen wisely. And it shouldn't be too long before you start to see the benefits of your choice. Once you do, you'll know you're on your way to reaching your dreams and achieving your goals.

Good planners are out there. When you find one, you *will* be able to change your financial life. I know you can. Hopefully, you're beginning to know you can, too.

SEVEN

HOW MUCH TO PAY A FINANCIAL PLANNER

You'll remember we mentioned the old argument about airplanes that goes something like this: one engine or two?

Basically it boils down to this question: When buying an airplane, should you buy a single-engine airplane or a multi-engine? Both types have their advantages. Single-engine airplanes are less expensive. Multi-engine airplanes, on the other hand, give you a backup engine in case you ever need it. If one engine goes out, there's a second one that can take over.

Put the question to some pilots, and you'll hear a few of them say, "Oh, no, no. You don't need two engines because engine failure is so rare. Even when it happens, it's usually the result of a pilot error and has nothing to do with the engine at all. So, having two engines doesn't do you any good because it was usually the pilot's fault anyway."

That settles it, right? After all, if engines rarely go out, why not save your money and buy a plane that costs less, needs less maintenance, and consumes less fuel?

Well, imagine this. You're flying in a single-engine airplane. You've got your spouse, your kids, and even your dog with you. You're flying over the Rocky

Mountains, which means you're so high up, you're "in the soup" as pilots call it. Flying straight through the clouds.

Suddenly, your plane starts to shudder. You hear funny noises outside the window. The engine is sputtering.

And then it goes out.

How much would you be willing to pay for a second engine right at that very moment? A million dollars? Ten million? How about *everything you own*, except your spouse, kids, and the dog?

Actually, you'd probably be willing to give the dog up, too.

The point is, there's really nothing you wouldn't do, and nothing you wouldn't pay, to have a second engine if your first one goes out. I don't care who you are or what your situation is. Unless you've got a death wish, you'd give everything for that second engine. So, ask yourself: "Would I rather pay a little more for it up front or pay *everything* when it's already too late?"

Like every other decision we make in life, it all comes down to what you really care about. What's truly important to you? Do you care about being safe, about staying alive, about taking care of your family? Or, do you care about saving a short-term buck?

Now apply that analogy to your financial plan. If the items in your plan are important to you, like your retirement, your health, or your savings, would you rather pay a bit more up front to protect them now or pay everything when it's already too late? Don't think of it as a hypothetical: answer it as if you had to choose *right now*.

I think we both know the answer.

I'm often asked the question, "Wes, how much does it cost to do all this? How much does it cost to create a plan?" Usually it's one of the first things out of a potential client's mouth. But it's not really the right question to ask. The right question is this: "What value am I getting out of all this?" or "What are all the things my money is going to get me?" The reason those are better questions to ask is that, again, the decisions we make ultimately aren't based solely on how much it will cost. Or at least they shouldn't be. They *should* be based on what you care about. We don't earn or hoard money just for money's sake. We earn money as a means to achieve our goals. If your goal is to retire or to protect your family in the event of a crisis or to start your own business or to travel or whatever, then it's less about how much it will cost you and more about whether your plan will get you there. In the end, what's more important? Your money or your goals? Aren't your goals what money is *for*?

To put it another way, a multi-engine plane will cost more than a single-engine plane, but what's more important? Your money or your life? What good is your money if you never put it to good use, if you never use it to achieve what's most important?

Now, that's not to say you shouldn't be conscious about the money you're spending on your plan. Most people, when they shop for something, are overly concerned about price. They ask questions like, "Am I paying the lowest price possible?" or "Can I find a lower price somewhere else?" or "How can I save money on this?" Many professionals in the financial services industry typically talk about price as well because they know that's what stirs people up. Banks do it; stockbrokers do it; a lot of people do it. Price trumps quality. They don't focus on what they're actually giving you. They don't focus on answering your questions.

I look at it a different way. It's all about asking yourself the following questions: "Am I getting the most bang for my buck?" "Am I buying the best product possible, or is there something better?" "Could I be getting more value from my money?"

Keep in mind that you are paying a financial planner for her experience. You're paying her to present you with options and alternatives, to have the know-how to answer your questions. So, choosing a financial planner is not about who will charge you the least, but about who will give you what you need to know to accomplish what you want to do. That's the value you're looking for; that's what you're paying for.

People who overlook value for the sake of price oftentimes *think* they're getting what they want, only to realize later they were mistaken. They think they've found a solution to their problem, and maybe they have, for a little while. But whether the problem is related to their investments, their taxes, their insurances, or their estate, low-cost solutions usually end up being short-term solutions. Eventually, the problem they were trying to fix comes back, and they have to spend even *more* money fixing it a second time. A quality financial plan, on the other hand, will save you money in the long run. Or, more accurately, it will help you achieve more with the money you have because that's what it's designed to do. When I do a plan, I make sure it provides long-term solutions for *every* aspect of your finances, and *that's* what saves you money. Cheap plans usually don't help you achieve much. Even though you saved a buck at first, it ultimately was a *waste* of money because it didn't do anything for you.

Again, you get what you paid for. Being cheap means getting cheap back.

How do you determine if you're getting the maximum amount of value for your money? There are two basic ways.

SHOP AROUND

Not all financial planners are created equal. In fact, some people who call themselves financial planners aren't planners at all. (We covered this in chapter 6.) That's why it's so important to visit several different planners—I'd say at least three—to see what they offer. And not just what they offer but who they are as people, and how they work. Do they perform tax planning as part of your overall plan? Do they execute your investments? Do they model your estate? Do they spend time to learn about you personally, about what makes you tick? Do they take note of your goals and values? Do they make sure they understand them? Are they looking at the roadblocks that could prevent you from reaching your goals? Do they spend equal time on both your retirement plan and your day-to-day living? Do they have a team of professionals to help you implement the plan?

If they don't do any of these things, *that's* when you should start getting nervous about the price. Don't just look at price and think you're comparing apples to apples. First, look to see if each planner just helps you with one aspect of your finances, like investments or taxes. Do they prepare a holistic plan that covers *all* of it? That's how you shop around. As you know by now, your investments affect your taxes, and your taxes affect your estate plan, and so on.

Next, how dedicated does each planner seem to his or her craft? Good planners should be consulting with other professionals (provided they've asked your permission), like other tax specialists or lawyers, in order to constantly perfect your plan. Obviously, consultations aren't necessary in every situation, but say you're an expatriate moving abroad. There are going to be some intricate tax consequences involved. When something like this happens, your planner should be ready and willing to consult with a specialist. This is the kind of dedication and commitment you should be looking for.

KNOW WHAT TO EXPECT

To determine whether you're getting enough value, know exactly what to expect before you meet with a planner. At my business, we have a sample plan we can review with any prospective clients the moment they walk through the door. It covers all the different areas we help you plan for—taxes, investments, retirement, estate planning, education funding, cash flow, and so on. (We reviewed most of these in chapters 3–5.) With a sample plan, we enable our clients to see exactly what they're getting from us. They can feel it, hold it in their hands, and use it as a point of reference on which to base their questions during our first meeting. So, when *you* shop around, ask each planner for a sample plan to look at. If it seems comprehensive, if it covers the same points we cover in this book, then you can feel certain you're getting a good financial plan. And a good financial plan is like that second engine: be willing to pay a little more now so you don't have to pay more to correct things later. Choose your planner based on *value* instead of price, and you won't ever regret it.

One other quick point about sample plans: a sample plan is similar to a show home. It's the best way for you to make sure the planner actually *does* all the things he or she promises, instead of just talking about them.

Now, if a planner doesn't have a sample plan available, ask her to prepare one for you. Tell her you're willing to wait for a few days while she puts it together. If she doesn't want to do that, then cross her off your list and start looking elsewhere. That's just not a good sign. It shows the planner isn't interested in you. She's not interested in providing what *you* want and need, and her attitude will probably extend to your actual plan. She'll try to fit you into some box and refuse to customize your plan because she's not interested in you; she just wants your money. She just wants to process your name, cash your cheque, and say, "Next!"

Planners like this aren't planners at all, and they should be avoided like the plague, even if choosing them would be easier on your wallet.

Transparency, on the other hand, *is* a good sign. Good planners shouldn't just show you *what* they provide, but *how* they provide it. Ask the planner for a list of references to contact. Now, references shouldn't be trusted completely. Every reference on the planner's list will be someone he knows will give him a favourable review. But it's a good start. If you ask references the right questions, you should be able to get a glimpse into how much value they got from their plans. You could ask them about all the things that went into their plan or if they've started implementing it yet. If so, has it helped? How? Did their planner find out about their goals and values? Does their plan help them work specifically *towards* those goals and values? Did the planner do what he said he would do? You get the idea.

We've taken the idea of transparency a bit further at HSI Financial Group. Every month we have a conference call that clients can choose to participate in. Prospective clients can join in, too. We don't pick and choose who will be on the call. Participants can listen to clients' questions and concerns and can also hear them talk to one another. We provide opportunities for our clients to be transparent with one another, if they so choose, and we're quite proud of that.

We also host events for our clients that prospective clients can attend, too. That way, people who are interested in doing business with us can meet and talk to our clients and ask them questions like, "Does Wes do what he says he's going to do?" We do it multiple times a year. It's another opportunity to provide transparency.

That's what you're looking for from your financial planner.

There's a third way to find out what to expect from a planner, and it's probably the best of all. Consider asking him to read this book. I'm serious. Ask him to read the book and to tell you what he thinks. Does he disagree with anything? If so, why? Is there anything I talk about that he doesn't do? It'll give you a great point of comparison. If the planner doesn't have time to read the entire book, pick out some individual points and ask him to comment on them.

A FEW MORE THINGS TO WATCH OUT FOR

There's a bit more research you should conduct when choosing your planner and how much you're willing to pay for her services. One big question to ask is, "How much time are you going to spend preparing a plan for me?" Typically, you want the answer to be "two to three weeks." That's because

- there should be several meetings between you and the planner (face to face or over the phone) to cover your goals and values;

- it takes time for you to compile the information your planner needs;

- your planner should have ample time to research and calculate the projections that go into your plan;

- your planner needs time to actually write your plan; and

- revisions might be required after you've reviewed the plan.

If your planner intends on taking only a few days, I'd be wary. It's less important to get your plan done fast, and more important to get it done *right*.

Be especially wary of the planner who says he'll do something, but only after you tell him his competitor will do it. I've had many clients who have left their planners to come work with me because they see what we're providing, and they know we're providing what they want. When their original planner asks, "Why are you doing this?" they'll explain that the folks at HSI are doing more for them. Then, the planner will say, "Well, I can do all those things." But if this is true, why didn't he do them from the onset? The planners you look at should be very frank about what they offer. If they're not, and they appear too eager to agree with you to get your business, that should send up a red flag. Planners like that will only do as much as they have to do. In short, they want to do the least amount of work for the most remuneration.

Also watch out for the type of planner who says, "Here's three or four options to put your money in. You choose which one you want." That's not a plan, and the planner isn't providing any real direction here. Remember what we talked about in chapter 6? If you don't have a plan of your own, you'll become a part of someone else's, and you probably won't like it.

Ask each planner if his work ends after the plan is complete. Ask him, for example, if he does any follow-up work. Ask him, "Are you going to review my wills every couple of years or sooner if something changes?" That sort of thing. If he won't, he's providing less value for your money.

As of this writing, the Succession and Wills Act recently changed in one of the provinces where we practice. Currently, we're calling our clients to inform them of this change. We're asking them to come in for reviews, to see if we need to make any changes to their plan as a result. I guarantee you that most lawyers are not phoning their clients and telling them about it. You really have to rely on your planner to do that. That's value for your money.

For our clients, we also provide a series of "financial physicals" after their plan is complete. This is where we review their plan to see if it needs to be updated. We review their investment plan, their taxes, everything. Clients can choose how many of these they want to have. We always suggest a minimum of once per year, but it's up to them. The best part about it is that we call each client ahead of time. They don't have to call us, like it's a doctor's office. We keep track of where they are and let them know when it's time to come in for a review.

This is something that we know makes our clients happy, even the ones who started out by asking, "How much are you going to charge for this? I don't know if I can afford this." They realize now the price they previously balked at has a *lot* of value packed into it. The different fees and maintenance expenses that have been charged apply to far more than just their investments. So, they're getting the full bang for their buck, and it makes them feel a lot better. Later I'll ask them: "What do you think of the detail we've put into this thing? Do you feel we've done a thorough job? Is there anything we didn't do for you that you expected?" Usually, we get a very favourable response.

FEES

With all that said, let's discuss how exactly planners and other financial professionals get paid.

There are actually several different ways. No way is necessarily better than the other; what's important is that you're comfortable with it and that you understand it. Your planner should fully disclose how exactly he or she gets compensated so that there's no deception or misunderstanding.

The different forms of compensation depend on what your planner does for you. This is where things can get a little sticky.

We talked about this in the chapter titled "How to Ensure You Have a Good Plan." There are a lot of different terms and titles floating around the financial services industry—financial planner, financial advisor, investment advisor, stockbroker, wealth manager, and it goes on and on. There aren't really any strict definitions for most of these titles, and anyway it's not important what your professional calls herself. It's what she does for you that counts. Finding out *exactly* what she will do for you is the first step to determining how she'll be compensated. Just to keep it simple, I'll use the term "planner" to describe whichever professional you decide to work with.

The simplest thing you could hire your planner to do is to create a plan for you. That's it. Once he hands you the plan, you're out the door, and you never see him again. If you go that route—which I *don't* recommend—then the planner might charge you a flat fee. Other planners might charge you a fee at an hourly rate. The total you pay will depend on however many hours he worked for you. And that's fine—just make sure you ask the planner ahead of time exactly how many hours he thinks the job will take. And if it goes over, ask the planner to explain exactly how and why it went over.

The reason why I don't recommend hiring someone to create a plan for you who will do nothing else is that if you trust the planner to create a plan for you, you should also trust her to help you implement it. If you try to implement the plan yourself, it will stall. You won't be able to modify it if you need to. You might not understand how to do everything, and consequently parts of the plan won't get done. It'll become static, and so will you. If you hire someone to create a plan for you but don't hire her to help you implement it, you'll become a do-it-yourselfer. We've already discussed why that's never a good idea.

Remember, it's one thing to have a plan. It's another to actually follow it. That's where the best planners shine. That's why I stay in touch with my clients and why I schedule regular reviews. I don't just send someone away once I've created his or her plan. I check in. I make sure the plan is always working for my client—and that the client is always working the plan.

That said, there are plenty of professionals who will create a plan for you and nothing else. If that's what you decide to do, be prepared to pay a flat fee or an hourly rate. If you compare a planner who charges a flat fee to one who charges an hourly rate, and one is more than the other, ask each planner to describe what exactly will go into the plan. Approximately identical plans should cost approximately the same. But if the plans are *not* the same and one clearly has more value than the other, then you'll be able to determine which planner is honest and which is trying to squeeze you for extra cash. Again, neither *type* of compensation is better than the other. It's the value each planner provides that matters.

A word of caution. Some planners say they only do a plan, and it's for a fee, but then they channel you to an investment service that gives them a kickback or referral fee. This is not necessarily a bad thing, *provided* that your planner makes you aware of it.

On its own, a financial plan could cost you anywhere from two thousand to forty thousand dollars. It depends on how sophisticated the plan is and how complicated your finances are. If there's no question about the thoroughness of the planner, basic plans can be done inexpensively. More elaborate, long-term plans are going to cost you more. Again, your decision should be more about value than price. You always get what you pay for, so worry first about what you're *getting* before worrying about how much you're paying.

Now, let's say your planner does more for you than just the plan itself. Let's say she also manages your investments, arranges your insurance, and everything else we've gone over. I strongly recommend you hire someone who does this. Again, if you trust someone enough to plan your finances, you should trust her enough to manage them, too. Even more important, it's better to have your planner be your investment advisor, your tax planner, and so on, because that way, she'll be intimately familiar with your goals, your values, and how to fit every area of your finances into your overall plan. There won't be any question about whether the options your planner gave you are right for you; you know they are because she showed you how they fit *within* the plan.

If you hire this type of planner, her compensation is going to be somewhat different. You're not just paying for the plan, but for what she does *after* the plan, too. This could be in the form of fees or commissions or a mixture of both.

Commissions are what a planner receives every time he or she executes a financial transaction. Commissions can work nicely for you because you won't be charged every time something is done for you. For example, say one of my clients came to me with a question about his estate plan or a tax issue he needed to solve. We'd help him solve that problem because it's part of his plan. We wouldn't charge him for it because we were already paid a commission when we first handled his investments or set up his insurance.

In your case, if your planner makes a transaction on your behalf, he gets a commission. Now, commissions sometimes get bad press in the media because reporters and writers like to scare their readers about something called "churning." Churning is where your planner makes more trades than are necessary in order to generate more commissions. The media also like to harp on potential conflicts of interest. A conflict of interest arises when somebody motivates you to do something because it would benefit him or her—for example, if someone sells you a product when he or she gets paid a fee to sell that product. But potential conflicts of interest occur in *every* industry, whether you pay by the hour, by a flat fee, or by commission. Say you work with an accountant for whom you pay a flat fee. The accountant specializes in family trusts, so she recommends *everyone* set up a family trust, even when it's not appropriate. How you pay her has nothing to do with it; there's still a potential conflict of interest there.

Obviously, you don't want either churning or conflicts of interest to happen. And while it's important to watch out for them, you shouldn't let that sour you against commissions in general. That's just some members of the media using fear tactics in order to create a more dramatic story. They want more drama, more stories, because that means people pay more attention to them. So, sometimes—and you see this quite a bit in the financial industry—they'll blow problems out of proportion because it makes for a good story. I see the media saying negative things about commissions all the time, but what makes them such experts? They're not planners; they're not advisors; they're only journalists in search of a story.

Commissions are as valid a form of compensation as anything else. One variation on commissions is called a deferred sales charge, and it's a very efficient form of compensation. A deferred sales charge, or DSC, simply means that you don't pay any commissions up front after buying an investment or some other financial instrument. The cost is deferred. The way it normally works is that if you buy fifty shares of a mutual fund or segregated fund, you pay a commission up front. It comes out of your initial investment. But with a deferred sales charge, you don't pay anything until you *sell* the investment, whenever that might be. In most cases, the charge itself diminishes over time, depending on how long you hold the investment. It could diminish over five, six, seven years, all the way to zero. It's an extremely cost-effective way of doing business with a planner who's doing an extensive job for you because it would be very expensive for you to write a cheque for every service the planner does. Another reason I like it is that it removes the need to actually write a cheque every time. As I explained above, if your planner does a service for you, he or she doesn't have to send you a bill for it.

Some planners are compensated through fees. There are several different kinds. Some fees are basically an hourly rate, where the planner will charge based on how many hours he works for you throughout the year. Then there are fee-based planners who will charge based on a percentage of your assets under their management. So, if you have $500,000 in assets that the planner is advising on, and he charges a management fee of 1 or 2 percent, he gets 1 or 2 percent of that $500,000 as compensation for the advice he's giving. That can be nice because, again, you're not writing a cheque. The problem with fees, though, is that this 1 or 2 percent means you're working with $490,000 instead of the $500,000 you originally had to invest. Also, the planner might charge you 1 or 2 percent to manage your investments, but what if you don't require that much management? What if your plan—always the most important thing—focuses less on investments and more on taxes, insurance, or cash flow? You might be paying a lot of money for your planner to do very little.

The point is that there are advantages and disadvantages to everything. Neither fees nor commissions are inherently better than the other. It's all about the service and value the planner provides, and whether that's worth the price you're paying. What we do at HSI is make our clients an offer. We tell people that we can do it either way they want. We'll charge a fee if they want to go the fee route, or we'll go a commission route if they want to go the commission route. Typically, the commission route is far more cost-effective for them, and we'll waive any fees if they transfer a certain amount of assets under our care. But we're giving the client options. We're being open and disclosing exactly how we're getting paid. And we're not taking sides; we're not being biased by choosing one route and then bashing the other in order to scare prospective clients from going with one of our competitors.

That's another thing to watch out for. People get so hung up on commissions versus fees because they're being misguided by somebody else's opinion, and that opinion is designed to channel you into the direction they want you to go. Everybody does it. Banks do it. Stockbrokers do it. Investment advisors do it. They try to make you sensitive to their competitors' way of doing business. A bank will say to you, "You know, you're paying all these deferred sales charges and maintenance fees, and that's just way too much." Then, the public gets ahold of that and it pisses them off. They'll think they're being scammed or something. "I'm paying too much in fees!" But they never stopped to consider what angle the bank is trying to play. They don't look at the big picture. For example, a bank might take your money and charge you a lower fee, but that's because they're *giving* you less. They may say they're charging less for investment advice, but they're not really giving you investment advice. They're just putting your money somewhere, regardless of whether it fits in with your plan or not. You might even say they're putting you into *their* plan. If you really look at it, you might be paying less money in terms of total dollars, but you're paying *more* relative to what you're actually getting, while still wandering aimlessly. You're paying more for less. Some banks even have the same fees as independent planners do. With those banks, you're *definitely* paying more for less.

Whenever I get new clients who are switching over to me, I hear these kinds of questions. They'll say, "Wes, I was over at the bank the other day, and the bank says I would be paying too much if I use your services." My response is, "OK, well, what exactly are you looking at? What did the bank compare? What have they been doing for you? What has their service been like compared to mine? What are you getting from them compared to what you're going to get with us?" After they think about it, they realize the point I'm making. If all their bank can say against us is that they'll be paying more in fees, that's a really weak argument. It's usually not even true. The bank charges plenty of fees of their own. The difference is, we offer more for our clients' money than they do.

So, why did they ask these questions? Because somebody planted it in their head to start worrying about what they're *paying* instead of what they're *getting*. Someone planted it in their heads that commissions are bad or fees are bad. If anyone does that to you, I'd consider that a major red flag. I'd be leery of anyone who's using the fee or the commission angle to convince you to become a client.

One more word of caution. Sometimes people actually pay more for financial services than they realize, which is another reason why transparency is so important; you don't want to ever get into a situation where you *think* you're only paying a fee, but you're also paying commissions as well (or vice versa). Too many banks and financial institutions pretend like you're basically paying nothing for their services, but *everyone* gets paid. No one is going to help you for free. So, if the price you're paying ever seems too good to be true, watch out. You might be paying more than you think you are. If a financial planner is truly good at her job, if she's *truly* concerned about giving great value, she should be using her *service* as a selling point, not her cost, because again, *everybody* gets paid. No one is doing his or her job for free. No one is doing charity work. No one wants to do more for less. And just as every planner gets paid, every client gets what he or she pays for. Being cheap means getting cheap back.

The actual price you pay for a financial plan will depend on the planner involved, on the part of the world you live in, and on other factors. But the most important factor is the quality of the job the planner will do for you, the quality of the plan, or the value you get from it. Don't be too concerned with overpaying for things and not concerned enough with undervaluing them. Certainly there are financial planners out there who charge absurdly high fees, but less time should be spent worrying on that and more on *whether your plan will do everything you need it to do*. Whether it's the mechanic you take your car to, the plumber who comes to your house, or your financial planner, the ultimate question is not "How much do I pay for his services?" but rather "Are his services the best I can get for my money?" Think about it. Imagine you've taken a broken-down car to a mechanic. When you get it back, it looks good as new, runs like a dream, and *doesn't break down again* for a very, very long time. Will you tell your friends, "Yeah, the mechanic was good, but he cost way too much money"? Doubtful. The farther down the road you get, the farther that car takes you, the more you'll say, "He was great—worth every penny."

The same is true of a good financial planner. The same is true of a good financial plan.

Good planners never cut corners. You shouldn't either. But when you're too focused on cost, that's exactly what you're doing. You're putting cost ahead of quality, which means you're putting cost ahead of your goals, your dreams, and your values. But is cost what you really care about?

If it is, forget it. You're probably not ready for a real financial plan anyways.

KNOW YOU CAN

Money is valuable. That's why people don't want to part with more than they have to. But a financial plan is not an expense; it's an investment. In the long run, your financial plan will help you do more with the money you have, which means no more worrying about having enough money for everything else you need and want. It means no more wondering if you can make your money last. With a good financial plan, you'll know you can.

That's why planning isn't about how much you spend.

It's about how much you get back.

EIGHT

INVESTING DOESN'T HAVE TO BE COMPLICATED

When they contemplate investing, many people think that it's only a game for the rich to play or that it's such a complicated process, it's best to just put your money in a savings account and leave it at that. Yet, investing doesn't have to be complicated, and it should almost always be a part of your financial plan.

Think back to the last time you flew on an airplane. How much did you know about the plane when you got on board? Did you understand all the laws of physics that keep airplanes up? What about the principles of aerodynamics? If you sat in the cockpit, would you have the slightest idea how to work the controls?

Probably not. And yet, you still got on the airplane. That's because you knew the basics. You knew enough to feel comfortable with flying. You picked a destination and then picked a flight that would take you there. Hopefully you researched things a bit and chose an airline that had a good reputation; you'd never fly with a company you hadn't heard of before, would you? You had a pretty good idea the plane would go up and come down all in one piece. You paid attention to the emergency procedures discussed at the start of the flight, so you knew what to do in case the plane had to make an off-field landing.

In short, you knew what you had to know in order to get where you wanted to be. The rest was in the hands of professionals—licensed, trained, educated professionals.

Not a complicated process.

Let's go back to investing. Another group of people, when they invest, will simply do whatever a perceived authority tells them to do. They'll choose products they hear about on TV or products that a "friend of a friend" told them about. They had no idea whether the investment was right for them, only that it was a "hot stock tip" that they shouldn't pass up.

Now, imagine you were getting on the plane, and you had no idea what airline it belonged to. You didn't have a ticket, so you didn't know where you were going. You expected a big, roomy jetliner, but instead you found yourself in a cramped little cabin. The only reason you got on in the first place was that someone told you to. So, all you could do was sit there and just pray you actually landed in one piece, hopefully somewhere in the vicinity of where you actually wanted to be.

But that didn't happen. You'd never fly in a situation like that. No one would.

Yet, when it comes to investing, many people do exactly that. Before clients come to me, they often make one of the two following mistakes:

1. They don't invest at all, or they invest unwisely, because they think investing is too complicated. They think they have to understand all the ins and outs, all the complexities, all the nuances of every investment. They're like people who refuse to fly because they're not sure how all the instruments work.

2. They don't understand the basics of investing. They don't understand what they're getting into and where it's supposed to take them. They just do what they're told, but they couldn't explain to you *why*. These are the people who get on a mystery plane belonging to a mystery airline going to a mystery destination, just because someone told them to.

Now, in some cases it's not a bad idea to refrain from investing. It's better to stick your money under a mattress rather than invest in something you don't understand. But the truth is, investing doesn't have to be complicated. *Investments* may be complicated, but the actual investing process doesn't have to be. You *don't* have to know everything. On the other hand, you don't have to be in the dark, either. It's good to know where you're putting your money, and what's more, it's *simple*.

That's where your financial planner comes in.

When I take people up in my plane, it's their job to know the basics, to know where we're going, how I'll be taking them, to listen to the instructions I give, and so on. But it's my job to know how to fly the plane. I'll inspect the airplane inside and out before I take somebody on a ride along with me.

My job as a pilot is much the same as my job as a financial planner. I don't expect my clients to know everything about the investments they're involved in. That would take years of study, training, and experience. That's my job. It's for me to understand the ins and outs of any investment we're involved in. And the same is true of any financial planner. That's what you're relying on your planner for. That's why investing doesn't have to be complicated. *You are not required to know* all of those things, and, in fact, you probably shouldn't even try. Too many people come to their financial planners, having gone into do-it-yourselfer mode, saying things like, "I need more ETFs in my portfolio." Oh, really? How do you figure? "Well, because it's cheaper." But is it? Are you sure? How do you know? "Because I read about it online or heard about it on TV." I might add, "Or because ETFs are the flavour of the day." But making decisions with only a little bit of knowledge—and thinking it's a lot—is a dangerous thing to do.

(Quick little note: once upon a time, Exchange Traded Funds, or ETFs, were new and simple to understand. But now that they've become the flavour of the day, and now that too many investors have poured into ETFs without truly understanding them, ETFs have become more complicated than ever. The point of this isn't to say that ETFs are bad, but, like anything else, you have to understand what you're getting into and why. You should never invest because something is the flavour of the day.)

When people say this sort of thing to me, I always reply, "OK, explain it to me. Explain what an ETF is. Explain how exactly it'll get you from point A to point B. Don't just say it's cheaper; explain *why*. Explain how it fits in with your overall strategy or what your overall strategy is in the first place." No one ever can. Yet, they still want to make decisions based upon the little they *do* know. For example, here are two conversations. The first is a real one; the second is hypothetical.

CONVERSATION ONE

Someone recently said to me, "Wes, we bought an investment. It's going down. So, have we lost money?"

"No," I said, "not until you sell it."

"Well, it's going down, so we want to sell it."

"Then you've lost money."

You see? That's the danger in making decisions based on limited understanding. The way the conversation should have gone is like this:

CONVERSATION TWO

"We bought an investment. It's going down. But that's OK because I understand that in the long run, this investment will pay off. It's designed for me to hold on to it. That's why I got it in the first place. It's a long-term investment for my long-term goals."

"Exactly," I would say.

Again, simple, right? Nothing difficult about that. Nothing complicated. The *investment* might be complicated in and of itself, but all the investor has to know is *why* they have it and *where* it's supposed to take them. Investors should also understand what makes an investment go up, and what makes it come down. Your planner should always help you to understand that. Knowing *why* an investment goes up or down helps you know whether that investment is still good for you or not. If it's coming down because of economic conditions, for example, then it's probably still a good investment. It's simply being affected by external forces. If it comes down because the company behind it is changing drastically, that's another story. It's up to the planner to keep you informed about what's going on, but if you know the "why" as well as the "what," you can better make tough decisions.

In other words, investors just have to pay attention and know the basics. That's their job. The planner's job is to know the ins and outs. So, even when the investment is complicated, the *investing process doesn't have to be.*

I mentioned there were two basic problems with many investors. The first is that people don't invest, or they invest unwisely, because they think investing is complicated. Conversation One illustrates this point. The second problem is that people don't understand what they're getting into but just do what they're told. They blindly follow, even when they don't understand why.

Conversation Two could never happen with people like that. Instead, it would go something like this:

"We bought an investment. It's going down, but I'm going to hang on to it. I have no idea why, but that's what my advisor says, so that's what I'll do."

People who say things like this usually end up getting burned. They'll come back later and say, "This is terrible. What happened to all my money?" They have no idea what happened because they had no idea what they were getting into in the first place. They didn't know if it was the right or wrong investment for them (which usually means it was the latter).

How do you prevent this from happening to you? How do you avoid the second problem? What's the secret to investing? Here it is:

Always be able to explain why you have an investment, why it goes up or down, AND what it's supposed to do for you.

In short, the surest way to know if an investment is too complicated is to see if you can explain why you have it. If you can't, it's too complicated.

Remember, this all comes back to having a financial plan. Your financial plan is built around your goals. Your plan is supposed to help you reach those goals. Your investments should always be chosen with that in mind. If your investments don't fit in with your plan, they're the wrong investments for you. Being able to explain *why* you have an investment is the best and easiest way to determine if it fits within your overall plan.

Follow this rule of thumb for future reference: neither you nor your planner should ever choose an investment simply because you're looking for a high return. Instead, your planner should choose your investments based on what you need to achieve your goals. If you know your needs, and you can explain why your investments fulfill those needs, then the chances are high that it's a good investment for you.

Even the most complex investments are nothing compared to an airplane. In fact, airplanes are so complex, pilots themselves couldn't tell you *everything* about how they work. But they could tell you enough. For example, if you ever flew with me, I could tell you exactly why I'm most comfortable in a Cessna 340, why I may not be as comfortable with an Aerostar, and why I'm not big on the DA 42 for where I fly. I'm not saying these last two are bad airplanes; they're just not right for me. I could tell you exactly why you were sitting in my particular plane and why I had chosen it to get you to your destination. Most important, I could fly it and explain what I was doing and why. That's exactly what your financial planner should do, too.

When you start the process of making a plan, your planner will recommend certain investments to you. Again, your job is to know the basics of those investments. Your job is to be able to explain it back to her. If you can't, ask her questions until you can.

- What goal is this investment supposed to help me reach?

- Why are you recommending this investment?

- What are the risks?

- What are the guarantees, if any?

- What are the alternatives?

- What strategy do you have in mind for this type of investment?

If your planner recommends Canadian bonds, you should be able to explain why, and your planner should be able to explain why she recommends Canadian bonds over American bonds or Greek bonds or what have you. When she answers those questions, try again to explain it back to her. If you can't (or if she can't explain it to you in the first place), then politely decline. You're well within your rights to say, "This investment seems too complicated, and I'm not comfortable with it. Let's look at something simpler."

That's it. That's all you have to do. It's simple. It's easy. It's a surefire way to know your investments are right for *you*.

Maybe investing isn't so complicated after all.

HOW SOME PLANNERS PICK INVESTMENTS

Many planners, myself included, will often recommend mutual funds or segregated funds. (In the United States, segregated funds are called variable annuities.) Before we go on, a special note on segregated funds. Segregated funds offer benefits that a pure mutual fund doesn't. Some of these are as follows: tax-advantaged distributions, various guarantees, creditor protection, and estate protection. This is all because they are administered by an insurance company. Consequently, segregated funds fall under the Insurance Act of the province you live in. These funds are definitely worth taking a look at, but make sure to thoroughly discuss the benefits with your planner so that you can understand when they apply and when they don't.

For the sake of discussion, we'll lump both types (mutual funds and segregated funds) together and call them "pooled" funds. Pooled funds are when multiple investors "pool" their money together, placing the pool under professional management. Funds like these have many advantages. For example, they allow people to participate in investments that might normally be too expensive for individuals to own. The pooled fund itself will also consist of a number of different securities rather than just one. This is a good way to diversify your portfolio. In other words, when you have money in multiple types of investments, you can protect yourself in case one type decreases in value. Basically, diversification follows the rule of not putting all your eggs in one basket, and pooled funds are a great way to do that.

The funds themselves are run and supervised by a professional portfolio manager. So, when you buy a pooled fund, you're really buying management. A portfolio manager is not a planner. All day, every day, they do only one thing: build portfolios by researching different investments. Since the manager is choosing investments on your behalf, you're basically paying him or her to do a good job. So, the question is, is the manager a good one or a bad one?

That's for your financial planner to answer. If he recommends pooled funds, it's his job to choose which managers to go with. In my case, I interview them. I have one-on-one meetings with the managers I work with. I rarely pick a manager that I don't have a relationship with. If the manager is the one making the investment decisions, I want to know what kinds of decisions he or she is making.

It's your planner's job to explain exactly why and how he chooses his managers. In this case, ask your planner the following questions:

- How long has this person been a practicing investment manager?

- What have her returns been like over the years? (Don't ask what the *fund's* returns have been; ask about the manager's because that manager might have previously been overseeing a different fund.)

- Will you keep the fund if the manager changes?

- What is your (the planner's) strategy, and how does the manager you're choosing fit in with that strategy?

- What strategy is the manager using? How will this strategy fit with my overall plan? (The strategy is important because the manager might not always be in sync with your goals and risk tolerance. This is why people sometimes become discouraged with pooled funds. The "buy-hold-and-never-look-back" strategy doesn't always work.)

Just as with investments in general, you need to be able to explain these answers. If you can, and if you feel comfortable with the explanation, great. If you can't, then it's not right for you.

Investments are a critical part of any financial plan. Just keep in mind that you *don't* have to know everything about them. Nor do you have to take everything on faith. Investing does not have to be complicated, so don't let the fear of it deter you. Instead, always make sure you understand *what* you're investing in, *why*, and *how* it fits in with your overall plan. My rule of thumb: treat investing like you treat flying. Understand the basics, and you'll soon find that investing, like flying, can help get you exactly where you want to go.

Remember: if you have a financial plan and are working towards your goals, don't try to invest with just the highest possible return. Always follow your plan. The plan should tell you how much you need to reach your goals: how much to earn, how much to save, and so on. If your savings and income just won't be enough, that's when it's time to invest. If your planner determines your investments need to make 6 percent for you to reach your goal, choose an investment that *safely* gets you 6 percent. Why take on more risk with an investment that could possibly earn 15 percent when all you need is 6 percent? This isn't to say you won't ever get 15 percent, but if 6 percent is all you need, that's what you should aim for. Anything above that is gravy. Hanging yourself out there, always trying to shoot for 15 percent, spells trouble. In some cases, I can invest a client's portfolio in a guaranteed product and get that client to his or her destination with little or no risk.

One last thing. Sometimes people allow themselves to be talked out of good investments and into bad ones. The best way to protect yourself from this is to know how much you need. If an investment is getting you what you need, then it's doing what it's supposed to. If someone else—whether it's a friend, family member, or even another advisor—tries to tell you that his or her investments are better, you can say, "How do I know it's better? Just because you say so? I *know* what I'm investing in is right for me. Prove that what you recommend is right for me." It will help prevent you from making bad decisions or from being taken for a ride.

KNOW YOU CAN

Many people don't know how to invest or don't know if they can or should. But if you follow your financial plan, it won't be complicated. No longer will investing seem impossibly complex. No longer will you have to take things on faith or avoid the process altogether. You *can* and *will* be able to invest in a way that's right for you, in a way that will help you reach your financial goals.

Now, let's keep going. In the next two chapters, we'll delve a little deeper into the fundamentals of investing.

NINE

TWO MISCONCEPTIONS ABOUT INVESTING

Of all the different aspects of financial planning, investing is probably the most talked-about. There are radio shows, websites, and TV programs dedicated to it, as well as dozens of books and magazines. Almost everywhere you turn, you can see stock tickers giving the latest market updates or advertisements from big financial firms offering to manage your investments.

Yet, as I've constantly tried to make clear, every aspect of financial planning is connected. They all work best when in concert with each other. They're puzzle pieces in a larger picture. And if you're not looking at that overall picture, you're going to end up with one hell of a mixed-up puzzle.

But most people—even professionals—don't see it that way. They look at your investments as a separate entity, like it's a sport, or a game most people can only dream of playing. And the rule of this game? To make as much money as possible. Consequently, few investment strategies are designed to fit in with your overall plan. In fact, what often happens is your investments end up *sabotaging* your overall plan because your investment goals aren't in line with your financial goals, even though the former should be working for the latter.

You can see the truth of this even in the titles some professionals use. They might call themselves "investment advisors" or "wealth managers" or something like that, and the name describes exactly what they do. They manage your investments. That's it. Some of these advisors might request to see your financial plan before they start working with you, but most of them don't, and I think that's a big mistake. In fact, if an investment advisor doesn't ask to see your plan or doesn't require that you come up with a plan, then I think he or she is being truly negligent. It's a complete disservice to the client.

To illustrate the point, I'll do what I usually do: tell a story.

A few years ago, I started meeting with a prospective client. We'll call him Donald. Donald was into his seventies when he came to us, and while he was an intelligent man, he was also shortsighted. During one of our meetings, we got around to talking about investments. He told me that he needed his investments to earn a return of about 10–11 percent. I gave him a funny look.

"Really?" I said. "Because according to your plan, you only need to earn about four or five percent." That was all the return he needed in order to reach his goals in life.

He didn't understand this. He thought that since there are investments out there that could earn him 10 percent or more, he should be involved in those. After all, ten is more than four, right?

I asked him: "What investments are you thinking about?"

I had a feeling I wouldn't like the answer, and I was right. As it turns out, he once came into a good chunk of money—over half a million dollars, actually. He decided that he wanted to have some income from that money to fund his retirement. So, he met with an investment advisor and ended up putting the money into a universal life insurance product, in the hope that it would generate $40,000 worth of income a year. The product he invested in was built around a number of different concepts involving alternate investments and leveraged schemes and so on. In other words, it was extremely risky. (It would have to be in order to get that kind of a return.)

"So, how's it working out for you?" I asked.

He beat around the bush for a while. "It's doing better now," he said.

"OK, it's doing better now," I replied, "but that suggests it wasn't doing very well before."

"Well," he admitted, "it didn't work out too well to begin with, but it's recovering now."

"Are you getting the $40,000 a year that you wanted?"

I knew the answer just by the look on his face.

In the end, he finally admitted it: his $550,000 investment had dwindled down to $116,000. That's a loss of $434,000! Most people don't see that much money in a lifetime, and it was certainly more than *he* could afford. So, clearly he wasn't getting the $40,000 a month he was hoping for. In fact, after I pressed him further, I found out he hadn't received a *single* payment yet.

So, yeah—ten is a higher number than four, but the thing about heights is that the higher you go, the further you can fall. Investments that earn higher returns are usually much riskier. It's like gambling in Vegas. You can usually get a lot more money when you gamble $20,000 as opposed to $10,000, but you can lose a lot more, too. The more you bet, the more you risk. It's the same with investing.

Donald ended up losing the bulk of his money, which could have been avoided if he had a financial plan way back when or if his investment advisor had required that he get one. That investment *wasn't right for him*. He did not need to get a 10 percent return; all he needed was 4 percent. That's it—4 percent in order to meet his goals in life.

See, investing is just like everything else in finance; it should fit in with your overall plan. That's why we try to find out what your goals are, what your values are, what you really want in life. Do you want a *chance* at several million dollars, or do you want to *guarantee* retirement? If it's the latter, a risky investment may not be right for you. A safer investment is probably where you want your money to be. You shouldn't base your investments on the return percentage alone. Instead, base them on your appetite for risk and volatility. By extension, base your appetite for risk on your age, your goals, and the status of all your other finances. A thirty-five-year-old multi-millionaire who dreams of owning a private island has the ability to take on more risk than a seventy-year-old who just wants to retire. While I wouldn't necessarily advise him to, he does have the ability.

So, Misconception #1 is that the best investments are the ones that promise the most money. Or, put another way, Misconception #1 is that earning a lot of money is the objective of investing. It isn't. The objective of investing is getting the money you need to supplement your other forms of income so that you can meet your goals in life. With a financial plan, you'll know you can.

It took Donald a while to come to terms with this concept. He had an attitude that a plan wouldn't have helped him; his investments just weren't working yet, but gosh darn it, they would eventually! He was almost defensive about it.

I said to him, "Look, in hindsight, are you telling me that if you had *known* a high-risk investment wasn't right for your age, and wasn't consistent with your plan, you would have still gone through with it?"

"I don't know," he said. "I really don't know."

It wasn't until I pointed out that his *wife* was basically supporting *him* that he finally said, "All right, maybe I should have looked at things a bit differently."

"What you should have done," I said, "was have a plan."

Just a quick tangent here, before we continue on with investing. Remember back in chapter 6 when we discussed how to choose your financial planner? One of the most important things to consider, I said, was that you have to feel comfortable with who you're working with. Otherwise, you should cut that person loose. And the same is true of financial planners. If they're not comfortable with their client, then they should recommend you find someone else. Otherwise, the plan isn't going to be as good as it could be, and it won't be executed like it should be. Ultimately, everyone's just going to walk away unhappy.

While Donald is a great example of investing for the wrong reasons, he also serves as an illustration of how sometimes a planner-client relationship just isn't going to work. Here's why:

After I *finally* got Donald to admit his investment was a mistake, he still didn't agree to make his investments a part of his financial plan. In fact, he still wasn't comfortable having a plan in general. I think the reason he wasn't comfortable was that he had this idea that a plan would lock him in, would restrict him from what he perceived to be all the great opportunities floating around in the world. Like risky investments promising a 10 percent return. He didn't realize that in reality, a plan would liberate him from the fear of the unknown.

"I don't know about this, Wes," he told me. "What if I don't like the plan?"

Read that question again. *What if I don't like the plan?* By this point, you should know the answer as well as I do.

I didn't try to spare his feelings. "That's a silly question," I said. "How can you not like the plan? The plan is based off what *you* want, what *you* care about. So, if you don't like it, then apparently you don't like the very things coming out of your own mouth."

"What does that mean?" he asked.

I said, "Well, the whole idea of a plan revolves around *you* telling us what you have, what you need, and what you want. That's your job. It's *our* job to then put it all down in a logical, readable format, a format you can actually see and touch. Then, you'll be able to see what your taxes are going to look like, what expenses you'll have, what income you'll need. You'll have a map to guide you to your destination. You'll be able to see if your goals are realistic. So, if you don't like your plan, then you must not like the destination you chose."

Now, as you can probably glean, Donald is a pretty stubborn guy. He doesn't like to admit that he's wrong. He started grasping for straws. "Well, you said it would cost a few thousand dollars to put together a plan. That's a lot of money."

I looked at him for a long moment. "That comment disturbs me, Don," I said, "because here you are complaining about spending a few thousand dollars, and yet you just lost over $400,000 in an investment you never would have been involved in if you had a plan in the first place. That was a mistake, but you still have time to rectify it. If you spend a few thousand *now*, you can make sure you never make the same mistake again."

But he still seemed skeptical. I almost wonder if he looked at investing like other people look at a trip to Vegas. Sure, it's dangerous. Sure, you can get burned. But it's *fun*. And he didn't want a plan to put handcuffs on his fun. I don't think he was really serious about creating a plan, and if he wasn't serious at age seventy, then he'd never be serious. He probably just met with me because he wanted someone to complain to.

At that point, I knew we weren't going to be working together. I just wasn't comfortable with him. I wasn't comfortable with his character, with his attitude, any of it. So, I told him. I said, "I'm sorry. I think you're a good guy, but this isn't going to work out. We'd better go our separate ways. My job is to help people resolve their problems. If that's not what you want, then there's nothing I can do for you. I don't want to hand you a piece of paper with some numbers on it that you don't even care about."

Ultimately, he didn't understand investing, and he didn't understand the value of a plan. You can't just put your money out there and hope for the best. People like that are like pilots who don't understand planes. Both end up going in the same direction.

Nowhere.

Now onto Misconception #2. For that, let's talk about Donald's universal life insurance product for a few minutes because it illustrates another point about investing that most people don't know about.

It might seem reasonable to think that, since Donald's investment failed so spectacularly, it was a "bad" investment. This is the kind of thing you hear in the media a lot: there are "good" investments and "bad" investments, like dairy products gone rotten. Investing, some would have you believe, is simply a matter of choosing the "good" investments and avoiding the "bad" ones.

At first glance, this might seem like a reasonable theory. But if you take a closer look, you'll see that it just doesn't make sense. Take Donald's investment. His universal life insurance product actually did exactly what it was designed to do. It was all the schemes attached to it that made it the wrong choice for him. But leaving that aside, what if it hadn't burned him? What if it *did* give him a return of 10 percent?

"But it *didn't*, Wes, that's the point," I hear you saying. And sure, it was definitely a failed investment. But suppose it worked. Would anyone call it a bad investment then—if Donald ended up getting a cheque for $40,000 every year? Of course not. People would be lining up to get on board. It's like saying back in 2001 that all dot-com investments—that is, investing in online companies—are bad. And while it's true that a lot failed miserably, you also had your mega successes. Google and Amazon eventually became huge hits, even after their rocky starts. So, to say that all dot-com investments are bad just isn't correct.

By extension, you can't say universal life insurance products are "bad" investments. With universal life insurance, you can choose specific investments under the insurance carrier's platform. You can choose stocks; you can choose bonds; you can choose a lot of things, and it's your choices that will determine your return. So, the product itself isn't "bad." And that's true whether you're talking about investing in stocks, bonds, ETFs, pooled funds, emerging markets, real estate, derivatives, you name it. Even extremely risky investments aren't "bad." There is no type of investment inherently "bad" or inherently "good," and it's that type of thinking that leads people to chasing holy grails or discarding potentially lucrative alternatives. The problem is that they limit themselves to thinking in terms of black and white.

In reality, people need to start replacing the terms "good" and "bad" with "right for me" and "wrong for me." Donald's universal life insurance product was a mistake—not because it was inherently bad, but because the scheme attached to it made it wrong *for him*. He couldn't afford the risk he was undertaking. *Risk* is defined as "the potential that a chosen action will result in an unfavourable outcome." In Donald's case, any unfavourable outcome was too big of a hit. The possibility of a 10 percent return just didn't outweigh the risk of an 80 percent drop. *Some* people can afford to take that chance, but Donald couldn't.

Now, let's leave the idea of "risk" aside for a moment. Many people—including a lot of professionals—use criteria beyond just risk to delude themselves into thinking some investments are inherently better than others. You have to be wary of this whenever you discuss your investments because this is usually where a person's biases leak through.

For example, an investment advisor might tell you the following:

- "I never have my clients invest in real estate. The money gets too tied up. You should always be involved in more liquid investments."

- "I only invest in simple things. The more complicated it is, the bigger the chance something could go wrong. That's why I never use derivatives."

- "GICs and CDs are bad investments. The interest rates are so low, they're just not worth it."

- "ETFs are the best sort of investment out there. That's because they're cheap and tax efficient. I recommend all my clients put their money in ETFs."

- "Don't ever invest in annuities because your estate won't get anything when you die."

None of these statements is farfetched, but each can be easily picked apart. Real estate might not be very liquid—that is, it's not easy to move your money in and out—but if you have *other* investments that are liquid, then real estate could be a good option for you. And while it's true some investments are more complicated than others, the word "complicated" is relative. What's complicated and hard to understand for one advisor might be pretty simple for another. GICs and CDs, meanwhile, can be a safe-haven for your money in troubled times, and while ETFs might seem cheap, they're becoming more and more complicated, and thus more expensive.

Do you see what I mean? When professionals think that some investments are "good" and others are "bad," they're putting all their clients into the same shoebox. That's incompatible with proper financial planning. Your plan is supposed to be *unique* to you, but how will it be unique to you if you're investing your money according to what everyone else is doing? It just doesn't make sense.

Be on the lookout for blanket statements or black-and-white thinking. Instead, take each investment type one at a time, deciding not if it's good or bad… but if it's right for *you*.

So, these are the two biggest misconceptions about investing: that it's all about getting the highest return possible, and that some investments are better than others. Instead, investing is about getting you what you need. It's about using *your* goals and *your* values to determine where to put your money.

Once you understand the truth, you'll realize that these two points actually work in tandem. Remember:

A financial plan is a map, unique to you, designed to get you to your destination in a way that helps you stay realistic and focused.

Why am I saying this again? Because the same rule applies to investing. Your investments are not solely about making you a ton of money, and you shouldn't choose them based on a rigid outlook of what's good or bad. Your investments are there to help you get to your destination, and you should choose them according to criteria *unique to you*.

To sum it all up: a true financial plan should *never* be boilerplate. A true investment strategy should never be, either.

In the next chapter, we'll discuss what a true investment strategy looks like.

TEN

INVESTMENT STRATEGY

When choosing the person who handles your investments, ask him or her this question: "Who buys more potato chips, an eighteen-year-old or a forty-two-year-old?"

In fact, go ahead and ask a lot of people. Ask your spouse, your friends, your parents, whoever. I'm willing to bet that most of them will give the same answer: the eighteen-year-old buys more potato chips. If you press them on it, they'd say, "Well, teenagers eat more junk food than grown-ups do" or "Most forty-two-year-olds are starting to watch what they eat for health reasons." Some might even say, "Well, potato chip companies advertise for younger people more than older people, so it makes sense that an eighteen-year-old would eat more."

But they'd all be wrong.

Now, your average eighteen-year-old probably *eats* more potato chips than a forty-two-year-old does, but that wasn't the question. The question was who *buys* more. And the answer is the opposite of what you might expect. The forty-two-year-old buys more because he's not buying them just for himself. He's buying them for himself and his wife and, most important, his kids. The eighteen-year-old, by contrast, is buying only for himself. So, if you have kids and you've ever been to the grocery store, ask yourself if you buy more chips now or when you were in college.

We both know the answer.

Both the question and the answer are important because they illustrate an important part of choosing investments: fundamentals. Fundamentals are how you determine between a good business to invest in and a bad one. One of the key fundamentals is demographics. At HSI we rely in part on the demographic information provided by Dent Research. For example, say you are looking at a particular company's stock. Demographics will show you who is buying the company's products. Who is using them? What's the market? Is it an aging demographic or a younger one? Is it mostly twenty-somethings buying their product or a population that is vastly older? If it's the latter, how long can we realistically expect that demographic to be around? Will the company's products still be relevant after the current generation is gone?

It's an important thing to consider because it shows you the long-term prospects for the company, which in turn affects its stock. That, in turn, affects whether it's a good business to invest in or a bad one.

In the last chapter, we talked about how there aren't good investments or bad investments (provided they aren't schemes or scams). There are investments that are right for you and ones that are wrong for you, but you can't discriminate between investments by *type*. However, there are good companies to invest in, and bad companies. In this chapter, I want to spare a few words on how exactly to determine the good from the bad, and why it's important to have a *strategy* in mind when making that determination. Let's talk about strategies first.

THE IMPORTANCE OF AN INVESTMENT STRATEGY

There are many investment advisors out there who don't understand demographics or fundamentals in general. They base their investment choices on what's hot right now or when they think the price is low or because everybody else is doing something and they want to do the opposite. Those advisors might get good returns in the short run, but in the long run they will *always* experience losses. They're basically gambling, and their luck will eventually run out. But good investing isn't about gambling. It's not just about increasing the value of your money. It's not about blind greed. Instead, it's about having a *strategy* in place to pick investments best suited, with the least amount of risk, to help *you* reach your financial goals.

Of course, advisors aren't the only ones who chase returns. Regular people do it, too. I frequently have people tell me that their uncle or friend is an "investment guru," and that they've decided to put their money into an investment that their friend recommends. Investors who do this don't have any strategy. They haven't done any due diligence when researching the investment. There's no method to their madness. They're just acting on their friends' advice. Sometimes this works, and sometimes it doesn't, but it usually doesn't.

For example, I once knew a client who bought a couple dot-com stocks back in the midnineties. By 1999, she hit the proverbial lottery with these two stocks. I did a financial physical with her and suggested that she talk to her stockbroker to investigate possibly divesting from these two investments, in order to reduce her risk and secure her gains. But she didn't take my advice.

"That's something I'll have to think about," she said.

After some time, she came back to me and said that when she looked at everything, the return she had obtained on her own exceeded what her other investments had achieved with us. I agreed with her—we don't take an aggressive approach to investing. Even back then, we took a defensive approach, and we were quite proud of it. But from her perspective, these two stocks had given her a return of something like one thousand percent. But what she didn't understand was that it's not a real return until you secure it and reduce your risk.

She also mentioned that if she were to sell these stocks, she would owe a lot in tax. Again, I agreed because we had already done a tax pro forma and were well aware of this. If she sold her stocks, she should have had to pay $700,000 in tax.

"I've decided not to sell," she said. "I'm doing well on my own, so I want to keep going. And I don't want to pay the tax."

About six months later, the two companies she invested in went broke. So, I had to agree with her; in the end, she didn't have to pay any taxes at all!

If she had followed my advice and looked into putting her money into other, safer investments, she wouldn't have continued to receive an astronomically high return, but she would have *kept* the return she had already realized.

This story illustrates two important fundamentals of investing. First, you don't make investment decisions based on tax consequences. Second, you don't make investment decisions based off greed. If you are driven by greed, and you're always seeking big returns, it will come back to haunt you every time.

What we often see with people is that they like to ride investments that they perceive are doing well. These same people are the ones who usually refuse to invest in something that they think is going down. So, what happens is that they don't get *out* of investments when they should, and they don't get back *in* when they should, either. That's because they aren't making investment decisions based off their goals or needs. They aren't making decisions based on a strategy; they're just chasing numbers.

Whenever you hear someone complain about the markets, that's probably why. They got caught up in the hunt for a higher return, got bit and, as a result, got bitter.

Many prospective clients have come into my office over the years complaining about their investments. But the sad truth is that most of them only have themselves to blame because they never stopped to wonder if what they were investing in was right or wrong for them. They only cared if it seemed to be making them money at the time. In fact, whenever I challenge these clients as to what they were thinking, they usually say, "I don't know. I was just letting my advisor handle it."

"OK," I say, "then why did *he* choose the investments you're in?"

"I don't know" is the inevitable response.

"Well," I say, "what's his investment strategy?"

Here, I'll either get a blank look or something silly like, "He buys low and sells high." But that's not a strategy. That's just buying low and selling high.

"How is that working out for you?" I ask.

"Not so good, Wes. That's why I'm talking to you."

Now, the question I'd *like* to ask at this point is, "Well, how do you let this guy invest your money for you if you don't even know his strategy?" I mean, really.

Stop and consider how foolish that is. You might as well just open up your wallet and say "here, help yourself" because you're basically giving your money up on blind trust, and when has that ever been a good thing?

I get people all the time who don't know their advisor's strategy, and what's more, they don't even know if she *has* a strategy. For the sake of discussion, let's say she does. But if *you* don't know her strategy, then how do you know if it fits with yours? How do you know if her objectives are in tandem with your own? It's like hiring someone to build your house and then never taking the time to see how that person's going to do it. You might have a gorgeous image in your mind, but the builder you hired has a preoccupation with building the perfect house out of tin cans and shoe strings.

You would never do that with your house, so you should never do that with your investments. Your advisor's strategy—if she has one—might not be designed to help you accomplish what you want to accomplish. It might not take into account your situation, like your age, your income, and so on.

It's just a dumb situation all the way around, and it sure makes it harder for me to do my job because by then these people are sour on the whole process. What usually happens is that, after a person's first advisor goes broke and loses all their money, they'll scream that their investments were horrible and didn't do what they wanted them to do. Why does that make things harder for me? Because there's a good chance their investments were actually good ones. They just weren't the right ones.

Now the prospective client thinks that anything similar to the investments his or her first advisor chose are bad investments, which brings us back to the original subject: how to tell a good investment from the bad—or, rather, how to choose the right investments from the wrong ones.

CHOOSING THE RIGHT INVESTMENTS OVER THE WRONG INVESTMENTS

Generally speaking, there are good investments and right investments, but *good* and *right* do not necessarily mean the same thing. As said in the previous chapter, good investments are always right for somebody, but they might not be right for you. A good investment is determined by the thing you're investing in. The *right* investment is determined by whether that thing aligns with your financial goals.

When I create an investment strategy, my first step is to determine which are the right investments for my clients and which aren't. My way of doing so is not sexy. In fact, for most people it's downright boring. But it *works*. That is, my strategy isn't based purely on numbers. It's not based on what's skyrocketing right now.

Here's how my strategy works. First, I look at GICs, annuities, and other guaranteed vehicles. Then, I find portfolio managers who oversee pooled funds that I think will match the investment philosophy of the client and myself. Next, I'll interview the managers of these portfolios to determine if that's actually true. If the manager's philosophy doesn't fit my own, I won't invest with him or her.

I want portfolio managers to validate the strength of every company *they* invest with. Is the company's management good? Do they have a strong track record? Are they in debt? What's their vision for the future? What are they selling? Is their product a passing fad, or is it something people *need*? Is it something that's going to be just as important down the road as it is now? For example, I don't choose portfolio managers who invest in companies selling horsewhips. It's 2013. I don't care if the horsewhips are selling like hot cakes; they're just not important anymore. They're not current. That's not a good company to invest in.

By the way, a quick point about pooled funds. Although there are pros and cons with most investments, the advantage of a pooled fund is that when you sell it, you're not chasing the price down, as with a stock. You get the trade price on the day you request the sale. Now, pooled funds are one of just many great investments out there, and they're usually right for the strategy I've chosen. I want my clients to be able to understand that, to understand how pooled funds fit into our strategy and why I use them. Mutual funds are a type of investment that some investors are unhappy with lately, but usually an investor's anger is misdirected. It shouldn't necessarily be directed at the mutual fund or at segregated funds, either. However, it could be directed at his or her advisor. The investment is not the problem; the problem is the strategy or lack thereof. Again, it all comes down to the difference between something being a good investment, but not the *right* investment.

I always research the pooled fund to make sure it's largely in sync with my investment philosophy, that the portfolio has a good manager, that the investments inside are well-postured for the future. They actually create wealth. They have consistent revenue. They're not 100 percent research and development. They have good cash flow. So, as a financial planner, I can say with confidence that this is the right investment for my client.

That's half of my investment strategy right there. It's based on the same principle banks are *supposed* to have when loaning money to people. They look at the fundamentals of the applicant. Loaning a lot of money to a ninety-five-year-old isn't smart; the chances are not good that he or she will have the time to pay back the loan. That's demographics. Loaning money to someone who has great credit *and* time, on the other hand, with a track record of paying her debt, and who wants the loan to go to medical school, is a much smarter investment for the bank to make. (This was a big part of the problem in the subprime mortgage crisis that hit the United States so hard a few years ago. Banks started getting caught up on potential returns and ignored the fundamentals of good lending. Customers didn't understand the details of the loan, either. At some point, those loans would go from subprime to prime plus, meaning their interest rate would go up. Eventually, it caught up with both of them.)

Here's why I don't take the sexy approach to investing. When people come to me, they often bring me hot stock tips. They say, "My friends are in this, and they're doing well." Or, "My cousin's doing great with this stock. He made a lot of money last year." Well, OK. But did your friends tell you how much money they lost? Where were they four years ago when the recession hit?

For instance, let's say a client's cousin had $100,000 in 2008. Then the value went down to $50,000. They've yet to recover fully, but the cousin points to the 30 percent increase he got last year as proof that he's doing the right thing. But in order to recover, he would have to go up 100 percent of $50,000 to get back to $100,000. A 30 percent increase only brings him up to $65,000. Thirty percent sounds like a lot, but he hasn't really made any money; he's just not as bad as he was in '08. And, in many cases, the investments people are in *now* are the same types that got them into trouble in the first place. All they're doing is justifying their choices to make themselves feel better about a bad thing.

My way isn't nearly so exciting. In fact, I'm downright boring. I will try to avoid investments that can take my clients on a roller coaster ride. On the other hand, if my clients started out with roughly $100,000 in 2008, then they're still at $100,000 four years later or perhaps even up to $105,000. Maybe that doesn't sound impressive, but ask yourself this question: Which situation would *you* rather be in? Do you want to be up 30 percent this year, but lower than when you started? Or, would you prefer to get just 1 percent this year, but still be above six figures? Is it more important to have a higher percentage to brag about, or would you rather have more money?

When you pose the question like that, everybody would take the second option. But the problem is, most people don't think of it that way. Instead, they hear advisors saying, "I made thirty percent last year," whereas someone focused on the fundamentals made only 1 or 2 percent. But what Mr. 30 percent doesn't tell you is that he *lost* 50 percent the year before, and too many investors don't ask. They get caught up in the numbers, on short-term returns. They're not looking at the big picture.

My investment strategy is conservative because I look at the big picture. We don't position ourselves using a crystal ball because there's no such thing. The big picture is the only reliable tool we really have, and too often it's not as rosy as a lot of people think it is.

Take Greece, for instance. They're a good example. At the time of this writing, it was reported that the European Union is giving Greece another big, fat bailout to help them pare down their debt. At the same time, Greece started imposing more austerity measures, meaning a reduction in government spending on public services. So, a lot of "experts" started cheering and patting each other on the back because this was such great news. It meant Greece wasn't going to become insolvent. They weren't going to have to leave the European Union and go back to their old currency and cause a lot of ruckus in the financial world. Disaster averted! But that's just another example of failing to see the big picture. People got so caught up in the short term that they ignored the fact that it's this type of thinking that got Greece into trouble in the first place. They're trying to stave off disaster, but they're only slapping bandages on the problem. They're just repeating the same mistakes as before. Eventually, they're going to run out of bandages.

I didn't get too starry-eyed about Greece because I looked at the big picture. I looked at their fundamentals. Here, you've got a nation that is basically broke. They're in debt. Not good. Their demographics aren't good, either; they have a very old population, and it's only getting older, which means less people working and less innovation. Remember, you don't loan money to your ninety-five-year-old uncle who doesn't have a job. He's probably not going to pay you back in his lifetime. And Greece's management track record isn't so good either; they've had dysfunctional governments and a weak economy going back two hundred years. So, tell me...why should I get excited about Greece, again?

That's the first half of my investment strategy. It's about choosing *good* investments. It's not about short-term returns. It's about fundamentals. It's about choosing investments that work for you long term and won't come back to haunt you. Investments aren't supposed to be about gambling; they're supposed to be about *investing*.

CHOOSING THE RIGHT INVESTMENTS

The second half of my investment strategy is choosing the *right* investments. Remember, an investment may be good, but it may not be right. The right investments are dictated by your financial plan, and that's why any investment strategy must be a cog in your overall plan. It can't be a separate thing because it's *not* a separate thing. It affects, and is affected by, every other aspect of your finances.

We talked in the last chapter about why good investments sometimes fail—because they weren't the right investments. For example, a lot of people think that all speculative investments are bad, but that isn't necessarily true. Speculative investments are good investments if the underlying fundamentals are good. Let's go back to Greece. Investing in Greece would certainly be considered speculative because you're basically just gambling on Greece making a comeback. (After all, they have to bottom out at some point, right?)

Now, let's compare Greece to a fictional country. Let's name our country Phrygia, after an ancient kingdom located not too far from Greece.

Like Greece, Phrygia is a small country. It was a pretty empty place for a long time, but recently it's been re-settled. They've got a tiny economy, definitely a speculative investment. On the other hand, Phrygia has a very young population. They're new and they've got very little debt. Their president, a charismatic man, has been democratically elected, and the elections were deemed free and fair by outside observers. Recently, a new fuel source has been discovered there that seems very promising.

Now, this is all extremely simplistic, but hopefully you see the point. Both countries would be extremely speculative investments, but unlike Greece, Phrygia has some things going for it. It has decent fundamentals. So, while both countries are speculative, one could be a good investment; the other is definitely not.

Still, for many people, investing in Phrygia wouldn't be right. There's too much uncertainty. Because Phrygia is so young, they might be conquered by a neighbouring country or their new fuel source won't pan out or their president could turn out to be a dictator. There's the possibility of great returns there, but also great losses. That's why it's speculative. It's not for everybody. It's a good investment, but it's not always the right investment. In other words, if you are somebody who can't *afford* to handle big losses, investing in Phrygia is not for you. But if you're somebody who *can* afford it, then Phrygia would be pretty darn intriguing.

How do we choose the right investments? First, we start with a solid foundation. We don't put the cart before the horse. We need some kind of safety net, something that we know will always be there. A form of protection. Maybe it's emergency funds, an aggressive savings program, or guaranteed investments that provide a small, but certain, return. Maybe it's all three. The point is that we have *something* to fall back on in case everything else in the world goes awry. Basically, we make sure we control everything we *can* control. We can't control what the markets do, but we can control how much we save. We can't control whether we'll achieve all our dreams, but we can control our basic needs. So, we take care of those first. That's financial planning.

Pretty simple, right? Next, we'll build on that foundation, but we'll still invest prudently. We're not going to layer ourselves with speculative investments right from the word "go." We invest the majority of your portfolio in things that balance a solid return with a solid risk level, investments that have good track records. Finally, we might look at some more speculative investments, but *only if you can risk it, both financially and emotionally*. For example, you might be someone who can risk putting $60,000 in a very speculative stock, if $60,000 represents only 2 percent of your entire portfolio. It wouldn't kill you if you lose it. However, if that $60,000 represents half of your portfolio, then obviously you would want to stay away. This rule applies no matter how much money you have. If you're someone who can't afford to lose even $1,000, then we *don't risk losing it*. We'll only stick your money in places that we know are safe.

That's how you choose the right investments. You start with the ones you know are *good* and throw out all the others. Then we choose the ones with the least amount of risk and volatility. If there's an investment that can make you a lot of money, and you can afford the risk, then we'll look at that investment. But if you're someone who only needs a bit more money to reach your financial goals, and you *can't* afford to lose it, then we'll look at other investments. It's all based on what you can afford and what you need. It's based on what it takes to reach the goals you specified in your financial plan, and no more. That's the difference between investing and gambling. A prudent person doesn't gamble with his or her retirement savings.

Everyone wants more money, but no one wants to lose money. Whenever I do public presentations, I illustrate this point by proposing a bet to the audience. I take out a coin and say, "I'll make you a bet. I'll flip this coin with any one of you. We'll each choose a side. If you win, I will pay you twenty thousand dollars in cash right now. But if you lose, you're going to give me ten thousand. Who's in?"

Inevitably, people grin and shift in their seats and look around. They all like the sound of making $20,000, but none of them are willing to risk losing $10,000. I've had one guy in twenty years who took me up on it. He was trying to be clever. "I'm in," he said.

"All right," I replied. "Then show me the colour of your green, and we'll flip the coin right now. I'll put twenty thousand dollars on the table, and you do the same with your ten thousand dollars. Ready?"

He immediately sat down. In fact, he didn't say another thing for the rest of the night.

So, everyone wants more money, but no one wants to lose any. That consideration trumps everything else. And it should be the main focus of your investment strategy: always ensure you don't lose what you already have because investing is *not* supposed to be like gambling. It's not about going all in and hoping you walk away a winner. It's about being prudent and intelligent. It's about supplementing your finances in order to reach your goals in life.

To do that, you have to have a strategy, and your strategy should always be a part of your overall plan.

KNOW YOU CAN

The average investor can't interview company executives, and she can't usually talk with portfolio managers, either. But your financial planner can. So, with a financial plan, you know that the investment recommendations you're getting are coming from experts in the industry. A good portfolio manager will pick good businesses to invest with, and a good financial planner will choose good managers. So, if *you* pick a good planner, then you're well on your way to having good investments.

It all comes down to having a strategy. A proper investment strategy is a *big* part of getting to where you want to go. Without a financial plan, you don't have one. But when you create a plan, you will.

ELEVEN

MAKING GOOD FINANCIAL DECISIONS

One of the greatest things about creating a plan is that it teaches you how to make good financial decisions. How? A plan forces you to decide what you really care about. Determining what you really want out of life is the first step to making good financial decisions. Those who don't have their values in order, on the other hand, often make bad financial decisions.

Imagine this scenario:

You're on a plane. As you're sitting in your seat, reading a magazine, you hear the pilot's voice on the intercom.

"Ladies and gentlemen, this is the captain. I have some bad news. We only have twenty more minutes of fuel. We are going to have to make an emergency landing. Now, there is a long dirt strip just a few miles away that we could land on, but I've decided to fly into those mountains ahead in the hopes of finding an airport. So, sit back and enjoy your flight."

What would you think?

I know what you *should* think. The pilot is nuts. Doesn't he know that simply *landing* the plane is the most important thing? Why would you put off landing now just because there *might* be something better down the road? Why would you make a decision based not off what you *know*, but what you hope? Why would you give up your best chance at what you truly want the most?

Of course, the pilot knows that living is the most important thing, but he's never really *thought* about it like that. So, he makes bad decisions.

Fortunately, most pilots would never do this. But regular people do.

As crazy as it may seem, I see this mistake all the time when it comes to people's finances. Rather than base their decisions on *facts*, on values, on their current situation, people instead make decisions based on some vague occurrence in the future that they hope will happen. It's called a "wing and a prayer plan." It's basically like playing a game of chicken with your finances. If you care about anything at all, and I mean truly care, then you should never have a wing and a prayer plan. You should never bury your head in the sand just because you don't like the way things look now. You should never plan your future based off a "maybe." That's what the captain of our fictional airplane did. The results could be disastrous.

I'll give an example.

Over my years as a financial planner, I've met with many couples close to retirement. The couple in this story are really composites of a lot of different people, but for the sake of simplicity, we'll call them Sam and Marie. Sam was fifty-nine years old, Marie a little bit younger. Like most people their age, their number one question was, "Do we have enough money to retire on?" That was the only way they could think about retirement, in terms of hitting some magic number. Anything *above* the number meant they could do whatever they wanted. Anything below meant they couldn't retire at all.

I explained to them that it wasn't that simple. Retirement is more than numbers. It's about determining what you want out of life. What do you find fulfilling? What do you need in order to be happy?

At first, they didn't really get it. I had to ask them all sorts of questions before they understood, some from the scorecard we reviewed earlier. It took a while because as a financial planner, you don't always know what people will respond to. It's different for everybody. But I had shared with them that retirement wasn't about reaching some magic number; it was about choosing what you really cared about, and then planning how to reach *that* goal. Eventually the light came on. "Oh, we see what you're saying, Wes," they said. "We get it now."

Yet, it was still a struggle. They couldn't really decide what it was they wanted. They kept comparing their situation to mutual friends of ours. So, I said, "You know, here's how our friends are. What's most important about them is they are extremely happy. They're content. They're fun-loving. They're enjoying their retirement because they've achieved the things that are most important to them."

But Sam and Marie were skeptical. Sam said, "Yeah, but you've got to realize, Wes, that they look for bargains in everything they do. When they go golfing, they go to the cheapest golf course. They go to Happy Hour. Their life revolves around penny pinching."

I said, "Well, I don't think they really see it that way. What I see are two very happy people who are loving retirement. Going to the most expensive golf course isn't what they really value, when all is said and done. Neither is going to the most expensive restaurant. They don't care about that stuff. What they *do* care about is exactly what they have. The things they *need* to feel satisfied with life; that's what we planned for. That's what matters. If you *like* golfing on expensive courses, if that's what matters to you, great. We can plan for that. But the plan should be about what you truly care about, not what you think you should care about."

You should already be able to glean a little bit about Sam and Marie's personalities. They were spendthrifts, the kind of people who will get into debt to go on vacation. They didn't know what they wanted; they just *wanted*. That's why they thought in terms of magic numbers. Most people can't get the world when they retire, but they didn't understand that. It's hard to achieve goals when you don't have any. It's like our mythical pilot. He didn't know what he wanted; he just *wanted*. If he actually had his values figured out, he would have realized that just being able to *land* is the single most important thing. Everything else is secondary. Pilots can't afford to think like that, and neither can you, not when it comes to your finances, anyway.

Back to Sam and Marie. I looked at Sam and said, "You know, until you've decided what you want, you're not going to have a very content retirement, simply because you're always going to be comparing your life to somebody else's instead of living your own."

Their inability to have their own goals and decide their own values had already hurt them in the past. While working through the plan with them, they told me about a property they owned. It was not their primary residence, but it was completely paid for, and they weren't sure what to do with it. They had two options: rent or sell. Either way, there was a chance the house could provide them with more income than any other source.

"What do you think, Wes?" Sam asked. "Can we rent it?"

Many clients have asked me this sort of question over the years, and the conversation that ensued is one I've had multiple times with numerous people. "What kind of rent do you think you can get for it?" I asked. They came up with a number, and it was a pretty high one. I asked if they thought that was realistic. They didn't know, and I didn't know either. But it sounded a bit high.

"More importantly," I said, "let's leave the money aside for a moment. Is renting really what you want to do?"

"Well, if the money's good…," Sam began.

"Sure, but I didn't ask if you wanted the money. I asked if *renting* is what *you* really want to do. Being a landlord is basically like having a job. What happens if your renter demolishes your house and moves out? Now you've got to spend money to bring it back up to code before you can rent it again. In the meantime, you're losing income. What if the renter calls you in the middle of the night because the furnace is broken? Do you really want to spend your retirement working?"

They were finally starting to listen to me; their plan wasn't just about having a lot of money. It was about determining what they really wanted. Being a landlord was not something they wanted. Renting was out. Besides, after we crunched the numbers, we found that even on the high side, their rent money wouldn't have fulfilled their income requirements.

Next we looked at selling the house. But it wasn't a really good time to sell. The market was not kind to sellers at that point. Yet, that wasn't the case a year ago, when, as it turned out, they first looked at selling their house.

A year previously, when the market was still OK, they looked at hiring a real estate agent to help them sell it. They could have received a very good deal, but they decided it wasn't enough. And when I say "wasn't enough," I don't mean it wasn't enough to reach a specific goal. It just "wasn't enough" compared to their imaginary number, or compared to what their friends had. So, they tried to see if they could squeeze even more out of their house by selling it by themselves. That way, they could dispense with real estate fees and commissions to their agent, that sort of thing. Perhaps they also thought they could fetch a higher price if they did it on their own.

Whatever they thought, it didn't work. They couldn't sell the house for anything close to what they envisioned, meaning time passed and the market went sour and their prospects for a big payday got a lot smaller. I can't tell you how many times I've run through this scenario with clients and prospective clients. In Sam and Marie's case, they traded their present for a vague and uncertain future. They gambled on a "maybe."

They lost.

So dismissing their real estate agent and trying to sell on their own ended up being a bad financial decision, one that denied them a lot of money. If they'd had their values in order, if they'd realized that the money their agent could have acquired might have been enough to accomplish specific goals, they could have sold the house for a higher price than when they came to see me. Since they weren't working towards specific goals, they ended up shooting themselves in the foot. That's what usually happens when all you want is to see an absurdly high number in your bank account. As it turned out, the opposite ended up happening for Sam and Marie. They wanted as much money as possible, and they criticized their friends for being penny-pinchers, but when we started getting into the nitty-gritty of their plan, we found we had to start worrying about $200 here or $400 there. They had champagne dreams and a beer budget.

Next, they started talking again about renting, but it just wasn't going to provide them with enough money to live on. Selling was our only option, but they were unhappy that they couldn't command the same price as before. "Well, we could wait it out," they said to me. I said, "Wait *what* out? You don't know how long it's going to take. In fact, I think it's going to take quite a while for the economy to bounce back. In the meantime, it could even go down further."

I encouraged them to get a real estate agent to help them sell it, to find out what the net proceeds would be and get back to me, which they did. "It's quite a bit lower than we thought," they said. "Had we done it the first time, paid the real estate fees, had an actual goal in mind, we would have had more money."

After selling the house and investing the proceeds, I was able to help them get about $4,700 a month in income, which was better than the $1,800 they could have charged for rent. Not to mention the fact that they no longer had to worry about someone trashing their house or replacing the renter every time one moved out. They finally decided that one of the things they valued was peace of mind. They wanted to feel comfortable about where their money was coming from. Renting the house wouldn't have accomplished that. Selling the house and investing the proceeds did. So, even though they didn't make quite as much money as they wanted, it was enough to accomplish one of their goals.

That's what makes people happy. *That's* financial planning. And *that's* how you make good financial decisions.

Not long after I met with Sam and Marie, I helped another married couple nearing retirement. Their names were Terry and Clarissa. Clarissa was an easygoing woman who always found everything amusing. Terry was much more of a go-getter. He was different from Sam in that he knew exactly what he wanted, and he planned on having it. Setting goals, then, was not a problem for them, although setting goals and prioritizing them are two entirely different things. It was the latter they needed a bit of help on.

Then, too, they were similar to Sam and Marie in that they had a taste for champagne but a budget for beer. For example, one of their goals was to own a winter home in Arizona. This was a very important item for them, so much so that they requested a specific meeting just to talk about it. When they came into my office, we sat down, and I just let Terry talk. I think he already knew in his heart that it was a pipe dream because he said, "Wes, we want to buy this winter home, and I know you're not going to agree with this, but…" I just sat back and listened. Clarissa sat there, too, and the whole time she had this big grin on her face, as if she knew what was coming.

It was almost like a kid trying to plead with his parents for a puppy. At the end of his pitch, Terry said, "Wes, we're going to sell this and this and this and then buy this winter home, and we'll live in it six months of the year, and retirement's going to be wonderful." Now, this was an *expensive* winter home. It was big, had more bedrooms then they needed, and had all the latest features, you name it. When he finally finished talking about it, I just nodded. He looked carefully at me and said, "Wes, I've got to say that I really appreciate the fact that you didn't rain on my parade or blow this thing out of the water. But you didn't say if you think we can do this or not."

"Well, what do *you* guys think?" I asked. "I'm sure you've taken the time to discuss it. What's your opinion?"

But he didn't want to answer that. He kept on saying, "You, you, you." I shook my head. "It's not about me, me, me. It's always about you. How do *you* feel about it? How do *you* think it'll work into your plan?"

"Wes," he said, "I just want to know if we can get the sunshine home or not."

"Sure, you can get it," I replied. At that, his face just lit up. It absolutely lit up. "As long," I continued, "as you're both willing to work another eight or nine years."

Now, Clarissa's grin got really wide. She shook her head and chuckled. She already knew what her husband would say. She knew it wasn't going to happen. Terry said, "Are you sure?"

"You know the truth as well as I do," I replied. "You've seen the numbers. Do you want to run them again right now?"

He sighed. "No."

Terry was about sixty-two years old. Clarissa was sixty. They absolutely did not want to work until they were seventy. That was one of their values, too, and here's why not just having values but *prioritizing* them is so important—like the pilot who flies into the mountains. That's not someone who has his values in order. That's someone who sacrifices what he wants most of all for something he only wants right now. And to Terry's credit, he understood that. He wanted the winter home, but he wanted to be able to retire at a more reasonable age and have enough money to stay retired. Maybe he enjoyed drinking champagne, but he wasn't about to break the bank to do it.

I explained to him that for them to get this winter home, they would either have to work several more years or take $400,000 out of their retirement funds to buy it. "How do you think that's going to affect your income?" I asked.

Terry looked at Clarissa. "What do you think?"

"I don't think we can do it," she answered.

Terry wasn't angry. He just nodded. "Yeah, I see your point." It was nice to see him just *get* it. He didn't shoot the messenger because it wasn't the messenger telling him he couldn't get his dream home in Arizona. It was the numbers, and the numbers don't lie.

But now came the really beautiful part of financial planning. They had already determined that while they valued wintering in Arizona, they valued retiring in their sixties and having enough income even more. They weren't about to give up the thing they wanted most for something they wanted less, even if it was more tempting. But now we looked at the alternatives. Since travel *was* one of their goals, was there another way we could reach it?

As it turns out, there was. They decided to forego the really expensive winter home. Instead, I suggested just renting. Instead of blowing their money on a $400,000 winter home, they could spend much less on something just as nice. That way, they could still winter part time in Arizona and travel to see the world. Sure, it would have been nice to own their own place, the way some of their friends do. But what they *really* valued was simply being able to experience new things together.

So, you see the importance of values when it comes to making good financial decisions. What's more, I hope you see the importance of *prioritizing* your values. Terry and Clarissa dodged the bullet of sabotaging their own retirement by buying an expensive winter home they couldn't afford. They're happy. They're content because they were able to accomplish what *really* mattered to them, instead of what just *seemed* to matter. They stuck to their plan and made good decisions that they were comfortable with afterwards.

KNOW YOU CAN

Like Terry and Clarissa, you probably have goals, dreams, and desires. But, like Terry and Clarissa, you probably don't know how reasonable some of those goals are or what it will take to achieve them.

The financial planning process is so much more than just seeing numbers on a page. By working with a financial planner, you will be able to determine what it is you truly want, and you'll be able to see how much it will take for you to reach your goals. You'll see how much you need to earn, how much you'll have to save, and how reaching one goal will affect the other goals in your life. Most important, you'll be able to know exactly what *you* have to do to make your goals become a reality, instead of just a vague, hoped-for longing that may or may not ever come true.

Above all, the planning process will show you how to make good financial decisions. That way, whenever you want to accomplish something in the future, you won't have to wonder if you can…

You'll know you can.

TWELVE

INSURANCE

Insurance. Isn't it a loaded word? It often has a negative connotation because it conjures up the image of door-to-door salespeople or charlatans selling snake oil, people trying to make a quick buck by selling you items neither you nor they know anything about. And it's true—to an extent. There are definitely insurance products out there that you don't need and salespeople who will try to sell them to you. But insurance doesn't have to be a dirty word; in fact, it's a vital part of any good financial plan.

From a financial planner's perspective, insurance is a hard sell because most people view it as an expense. That's understandable. There may not be an immediate or tangible benefit to buying insurance. But viewing it as an expense is sort of missing the point of insurance in the first place. So, this chapter is designed to help you wrap your head around what insurance actually is, and why it's so important.

When I buy insurance, I ask myself, "Why am I doing this?" The first answer that pops into my mind, always, is that I love whatever it is I'm insuring. Mainly, I love and care about my family. One of the ways that I as a husband and father can show that love is by always providing for them, even if I'm dead and gone or sick or disabled. I always want my family to be taken care of. Period. Insurance is one way to do that.

That's the big secret behind insurance. Understanding what you love is how to decide which kinds of insurance you need and which you don't. Ultimately, our decisions reflect our values. Throughout this book, I've said again and again how a financial plan is about deciding what your values are, about what you truly care about. That's the theme of this book, and in no place is it more important than here.

So, take out a pen and write this down. Learn it. Memorize it. Make it a part of you. This is the secret. This is the rule of insurance:

If you can't afford to lose it, then insure it.

By this point, you should already have a list of your values. Hopefully you wrote it down, or maybe it's still in your head. But wherever you keep it, pull it out and look at it. Which things on that list can you *not* afford to lose? Those are the items that need to be insured. Most of the items you pick will come back to the same thing: yourself and your family. You can't afford to lose your life because of yourself and your family. You can't afford to lose your health because of yourself and your family. You can't afford to lose your house because of yourself and your family. You can't afford to lose the *belongings* in your house because…you get the idea. That's why the best insurance is the insurance you have in place when you need it, because losing what you've insured is just not an option.

A selfish person will have a hard time wrapping his or her head around the idea of insurance for this very reason. Selfish people don't see the value of it because all they want out of life is to please themselves. The only thing they *value* is themselves. So, most insurance products don't apply. This is a critical point because while I might still be able to *sell* insurance to a selfish person, I don't want to. I don't want to sell insurance to anyone. I want them to *buy it*. Not because I dazzled them with my sales pitch but because they *wanted* to. You're either the type of person who will buy insurance or you're not. You're either the type of person who loves your family or you're not. I can't change who my clients are as people, but it's *who they are as people* that will ultimately determine whether insurance is for them or not. If the values aren't there, they just aren't there.

For the sake of discussion, let's assume you're open to buying insurance, but you just don't know enough about it. Fair enough. Here's a quick rundown.

INSURANCE AND YOUR FINANCIAL PLAN

Now, you might be thinking, *"OK, insurance is important, but it's hardly something my financial planner needs to worry about."*

Wrong. It's a huge part of the equation. In fact, in many cases it guarantees the completion of your plan—for example, if you die too soon, live too long, or become disabled.

Remember, a financial plan is like a roadmap or a flight plan designed to get you from point A to point B, to help you reach your goals in life, both financial and otherwise. But a plan can't foresee the future. It can *assume* certain things, but it can't foresee. There's no telling what will happen to you down the road, but there could be road bumps. There could be turbulence. There almost always is.

Or, maybe it's worse than that. Maybe it's not a bump you encounter but instead a sudden drop. Maybe the ground beneath you gives way. Maybe lightning strikes your engine.

I'll say it plain. Your financial plan is supposed to get you from point A to point B, but sometimes things happen that physically prevent you from going anywhere. You could get sick and end up hospitalized for a long time. You could get injured and end up in a wheelchair, unable to work. You could die. And just like that, all the details of your plan get screwed up because maybe the plan was based on your earning a certain amount of money or retiring at a certain age. The goals you listed with your planner probably didn't include spending the rest of your life in bed.

So, what happens? You're in trouble, right?

Nope. And this is where insurance comes in. Insurance is sort of like a fail-safe for your financial plan. Even if something happens that you didn't expect, something catastrophic, then your fail-safe kicks in, and you can *still* reach your goals—or, at least, as many goals as humanly possible. Most important, your *family* can still get from point A to point B. Remember the story of Roger and Janet? After Roger fell off his roof, Janet had to work full time, leaving the kids at home and their financial future shot to hell. Nothing could have prevented the accident, but the effects could have been mitigated. Disability insurance could have kicked in—or Critical Illness or Long-Term Care. The money would have enabled them to achieve at least some of their goals in life. It would have given them a foundation to start again.

Insurance is a big part of any financial plan. We'll discuss how to make insurance as economically viable as possible, but first, let's go over a few different types.

DISABILITY INSURANCE

The Purpose: Disability insurance comes in handy if you become physically disabled *or* if you suffer from an illness and can no longer work. You can purchase insurance for accidents only or for illness only, but usually you purchase them together.

The Advantages: The biggest advantage of disability insurance is that it will *replace* your income if you no longer can earn income on your own. Some people think this kind of insurance is handy only if you have a career that might put you in harm's way or if you live a risky type of lifestyle. But that's wrong. *No one* is immune to illness, and no one is invincible. It doesn't matter if you are young or old, cautious or a daredevil. Anyone can fall off the roof or slip in the tub. It's not as if we know when those accidents will occur, either. Life is full of accidents that even the most careful people can't always prepare for. For that reason, disability insurance is for everyone. That's why it's valuable, and why you should have it *before* you need it.

It's also very handy if you're in a partnership. Let's say you own a small business, and you have a partner in that business. Normally if you become disabled or get sick and can no longer contribute, your partner would have every right to say, "Wait a minute, I'm the guy putting work into this company. You're not participating anymore; however, you still own 50 percent of it. So, all of my hard work is benefiting you." 50 percent of your partner's work would be going to you. That doesn't make much sense, does it? Here's where disability insurance kicks in. With disability insurance, you can enact a "buy-sell arrangement." (We'll talk about this more in the next chapter.) If you become disabled, one part of the disability insurance pays for your living expenses, while the second part pays out a lump sum, just like life insurance or critical illness insurance does. So, if you own 50 percent of your company and become disabled, your partner gets the benefit from the disability insurance to buy your shares back from you. That way, you get the money you need to move on with your life, and your partner becomes the sole owner of the business.

The Fine Print: Disability insurance expires, typically between the ages of sixty-five and seventy. There are two reasons for this:

1) Even if you're disabled, insurance companies anticipate that you are saving for retirement. They're also anticipating that you'll retire at sixty-five. Consequently, disability insurance typically expires at sixty-five when you would

be retired anyway and don't need to work. From the insurance company's point of view, it was only your employment income that needed to be replaced. How you fund your retirement is a completely different matter. But what about from *your* point of view? If you become disabled at say, thirty-six years old, and disability insurance is only covering your expenses, and if insurance is the only income you've got—and it's all going to expenses—then you're obviously not saving for retirement. So, when you hit sixty-five, you're in trouble.

2) The second reason is cost. Remember, it costs money to buy insurance, and the longer the term, the more it costs. If disability insurance lasted until people died, then very few people could afford to buy it.

The universal question, when it comes to insurance, is "So, when do I need it?" Disability insurance is always a good investment because you never know when an accident might occur. Just keep the fine print in mind, and you can ensure that becoming disabled doesn't have to be a financial disaster. This is especially important if a potential disability would affect not only you but other people, too, like your spouse, kids, or even business partners.

CRITICAL ILLNESS

The Purpose: Critical illness insurance is designed to cover you in case you contract one of the illnesses listed in your policy, such as cancer, a heart attack, the loss of a limb, neurological disorders, and many others.

The Advantages: This one is especially important in the United States due to the cost of healthcare. But it's just as important in Canada, too. We might not have to pay as much as Americans do, but we still have to pay something. Remember, in Canada, normal health insurance covers your nurses, your doctors, and your hospital stays, but it doesn't cover expenses. For example, if you get ill and can't pay your mortgage, critical illness insurance can help. Same thing if you have to convert your home or minivan to become wheelchair accessible. Normal health insurance doesn't cover those things, but critical illness does.

Critical illness insurance pays you a lump sum benefit if you contract one of the specific diseases listed in the policy. Generally, the list covers all the heavy hitters, like a who's-who of nasty conditions. For example, say you get cancer, like non-Hodgkin's lymphoma. Non-Hodgkin's lymphoma is treatable, and as long as you can *get* treatment, you'll probably survive. The downside is that you could be down and out for a year and a half or longer. Well, time doesn't stop during that year and a half. You've got things to do, debts to pay. Even if you have disability insurance, you are still probably going to have to burn through some savings just to get by. For example, you might have some big bill that just balloons on you. How are you going to pay for it? Remember, you're down and out. You're not working. So, critical illness insurance might be your only way to get by.

Or, let's say you get in an accident and lose a limb. This is where disability insurance kicks in, right? Well, yes, for the most part. But maybe you have to be in a wheelchair for the rest of your life. Maybe you have to change the access of your home to accommodate you. Maybe you've got to undergo rehabilitation. Disability insurance may not pay for all that kind of stuff, but critical illness insurance will. Unfortunately, some people don't qualify for disability insurance. For example, if you're a stay-at-home mom and don't have any income, you can't get disability insurance because disability insurance insures your income. You can't insure what you don't have. In situations like these, critical illness insurance becomes even more important.

Basically, critical illness insurance gives you the money to do what you need to do when your disability insurance won't cover it. Here's another example. Let's go back to non-Hodgkin's lymphoma. You need treatment, right? But what if you live somewhere in the Northwest Territories, where they don't have very good medical facilities? You'll need to go somewhere where they've got fantastic medical care, like the Mayo Clinic in Phoenix or Minnesota. That will cost you a small fortune and put a real burden on your family. It would even cost a lot just to go to Vancouver. Again, disability insurance isn't going to pay for that. But with critical illness, you get a lump sum *and* the ability to decide how to use it. If you signed up for a lump sum of $300,000, then as soon as you get sick, the insurance company writes a cheque for $300,000. You can do whatever you want with it. Heck, if you decide that you're not going to live to see another month, you could even use it to put on one *hell* of a big party.

The Fine Print: Some policies may require the policyholder to survive a minimum number of days after the illness was first diagnosed. This is called the "survival period." It varies from company to company, but the average is about a month.

Also, there may be rules as to what constitutes a valid diagnosis. It may need to be made by a specialist in your condition or after certain tests are done. And once you've made a claim on critical illness insurance, you sometimes might not be able to buy any more, or at least not for the condition you just suffered.

Over the twenty-eight years that I've been in business, I have had several female clients contract breast cancer and several male clients contract prostate cancer. One in particular that I worked with several years ago had critical illness insurance to help pay for her treatment. Before I first sold it to her, she and her husband were both somewhat skeptical. They were a young couple, so the thought of a critical illness seemed like a remote event, something that happens to older people, not them. They were too busy living their lives to worry about the chances of getting sick. But after reviewing the plan we came up with, they realized the potential importance of insurance, so they went ahead and bought it.

It's a good thing, too, because cancer is an equal-opportunity disease. Some forms might be based off genetics, but generally, it doesn't discriminate. When she contracted breast cancer, it came as a shock. Originally, she didn't even want to make a claim on her critical illness policy because it felt like waving the white flag, like throwing in the towel. But things got bad enough that they finally decided to make the claim.

So, the insurance company sent them the cheque right away. This was several years back, and she's still recovering now. Not too long ago, I asked her, "So, how are you doing?" She told me that things were going really well, with only a few little complications here and there. It's looking like she's going to be OK. She'll be a survivor. She'll be able to live her life almost as normally as she always wanted, as a wife and a mom.

I was thrilled to hear it, of course, but I was really gratified when her husband called me later. He said, "Wes, I just want to let you know how much we appreciate the fact that you recommended this kind of insurance." He said it made a huge difference in her recovery. Not only did it help pay for it, but it took away a lot of stress and anxiety because she didn't have to worry about not working or taking care of her kids. They were able to hire a live-in nanny and a housekeeper. All she had to do was concentrate on her recovery. That makes a huge difference to a sick person. After all, sick people have enough to worry about, right? They shouldn't have to worry about bills or anything else. Their health should always come first.

LONG-TERM CARE INSURANCE

The Purpose: Long-term care insurance, or LTC, is designed to pay for the cost of taking care of people who cannot care for themselves for a long period of time, either at home or in a facility.

One of the greatest problems we face in North America is our aging population. If you look at the demographics of the industrialized world, it's heavily weighted towards the more elderly end of the spectrum. But that's not all. Not only are we aging, but that aging demographic is also living longer. While that's great for them, it also comes with side effects. The more people there are, and the longer they live, the greater the burden on our medical system. Our aging demographic is already straining it to the limit.

To compensate, we need bigger and better long-term care facilities—more retirement homes, more extended care, more nurses, doctors, you name it. But all of that is expensive, and it's not going to get cheaper anytime soon. Just the opposite, actually. In fact, paying for *your* long-term care will eat up your assets and retirement funds faster than inflation ever could.

Go ahead and do some research on your own. Make a few phone calls and ask these long-term care facilities what it costs to house your grandma or your parents or yourself. It won't be a low number. One day those same costs will apply to you. It may even happen sooner than you think. If you're young, you probably think the only time you are going to go into a long-term care facility is when you're seventy-five years old and losing your mind or something. No, no, no. Even young people may need long-term care. For example, I had a relative who had a stroke in her midthirties and couldn't take care of herself anymore. And remember Roger and Janet? Roger was still fairly young when he had his accident. So, long-term care isn't just for the elderly.

The Advantages: LTC insurance can cover the costs of home care, assisted living, hospice, or nursing homes, among other things. It can be used to help pay for professional caregivers, therapists, private nurses, housekeepers, you name it, which makes it invaluable to you and your family. If you don't have professionals caring for you after you're no longer able to, the burden will probably fall on your children. It'll be a huge drain on their time, their money, and their patience. By purchasing LTC insurance, you're not only providing for yourself but for your loved ones, too. Remember what I said about insurance not being for selfish people?

Long-term care can also be a way to invest in your own dignity. If you speak with many elderly people, one of the things they really value is the chance to grow old at home rather than in a facility. LTC insurance can afford you that luxury.

The Fine Print: When purchasing LTC insurance, you have to be very, very careful that it's cost-effective and that you'll end up with a real benefit. What you and your planner will need to determine is how long you are paying for it, how high your premium will be, and if it's worth the benefit. For example, let's say your premium is high *and* you have to pay it for a long time. The benefit won't kick in until the day comes when you actually need long-term care. But what if you don't end up needing it until you're ninety? You might end up paying for LTC for twenty-five years but using it for only two or three. This shouldn't discourage you from purchasing it, but it does mean you need to give it some serious thought beforehand.

Also determine how long it will last. Many forms of LTC insurance last for a specific length of time. Others can potentially last your entire life, but technically last for a monetary lump sum value. In other words, the insurance will pay out the benefit over a period of years, but when the sum of that benefit is used up, it's over.

Ultimately, the question you have to ask yourself is, "How important is this to me right now?" If you're sixty and then end up needing long-term care when you turn sixty-one, then LTC insurance will give you a huge value. You get the benefit without having to pay too much for it. But what if you don't need it until you are eighty? You might end up paying for it longer than you'll actually be using it. The moral of the story? Weigh the benefits versus the cost before making any decision.

LIFE INSURANCE

The Purpose: Life insurance is probably the most well-known type of insurance. Basically, the insurance company agrees to pay the beneficiary a sum of money, or benefit, after the insured person dies.

The Advantage: The main advantage here is the simple but profound peace of mind you get from knowing your loved ones will be taken care of even after you pass away. Remember, death isn't a matter of *if,* but *when.* Here again is where we divide between selfish people and unselfish people. The selfish person doesn't care about what happens after he or she is gone: "I'm dead, so all of *my* worries are over." The unselfish person, on the other hand, thinks, "You know, I'd really like to leave some nice memories to my kid after my spouse or I am gone. I'd like them to always know how much I love them, even if I'm not around to tell them myself." You can do that with life insurance. Maybe it sounds a little silly, but it's the truth. It's a nice feeling for people to know that their moms, dads, or spouses took the time to make sure they'd always be taken care of.

Again, let's assume you're not a selfish person. The thing about death is that it's not the ending of the story. It's *an* ending but not *the* ending. The story goes on; it just has new characters. After we pass along, all of our loved ones are still living out their story, and part of that story is dealing with your death. So, your decision is a simple one: Do you want to leave behind happy memories or problems? Those who die without life insurance tend to do the latter, especially if they die young. What happens quite frequently when young people die without life insurance is that their children lose one parent and inherit a part-time parent. I'm not exaggerating when I say it often means that Mom or Dad has to take two jobs and is never home, or the oldest kid has to get a job to help support the family. I see these things all the time, and nobody does anything about it. *Death costs money.* A lot of money. And it'll be your loved ones who get the bill.

Let's get into the nitty-gritty on life insurance for a moment. Life insurance can come in three forms: term, whole life, and universal life. I liken term insurance to renting a house, and whole life and universal life to *owning* a house. When you rent, you have no equity in the house you live in because you give it back to the person who owns it when you are ready to move. But as long as you stay there, you have to pay rent. The same goes for term insurance. You don't have equity in it, and you have to pay for it for a period of time. When that period is up, you either have to renew and pay more or give the potential benefit back to the insurance company.

Whole life insurance, or universal life insurance, is a bit like owning a house (see the chart on page 125). You have equity in it. With universal life insurance, you can even pay it off, just like owning a house, and not have to pay anything else for it. There are other financial advantages to universal life insurance, too.

Life insurance can be used as collateral to help secure a loan. In most cases, as your equity is growing, it's growing on a tax-deferred or sheltered basis. This can be extremely advantageous for people who want to shelter their money without any other means of doing so. For instance, people who want to put their money away where it can grow on a tax-deferred basis can put it in universal life insurance for that very purpose. People who do this may not even *need* the life insurance benefit; they just want their money growing in a tax-sheltered environment.

Insurance policies like these can actually be split as well. For example, say your adult child needs life insurance, and you don't. You can split the policy so the benefit covers him or her, but your money, which is growing tax-deferred, stays with you. The cash value in the policy can then be used for retirement.

When you compare the two, it's clear that term insurance covers a short-term problem, while whole life covers a permanent problem. Both provide the same type of benefit in that, if you die, your beneficiary will receive a sum of money to help him or her recover and carry on with life. Term insurance only covers you for a specific period of time; whole life has no limit. (However, whole life will typically pay its benefit out at age one hundred whether you're alive or dead.) Term insurance might appear to be cheaper at the beginning, but as it renews, it becomes more expensive. Whole life comes with extra financial advantages, and you never have to worry about losing coverage.

How do you choose between term and whole life? Well, as with your investments, no one type of insurance is better or worse than the other. Some are better or worse for *you*, so in order to choose, you must first know what you need. What exactly are you trying to protect? How much can you afford to pay? It's similar to asking what's better, renting a house or owning one. It all depends on what you need at the time and what you can afford. Renting gives you a roof over your head, and if that's all you need, it's the best option. Owning a house gives you a permanent home where you can raise a family and do with what you like. One efficiently covers short-term problems; the other covers long-term problems, like retirement, and offers stability. The answer all depends on what you need and what you value.

Here's an example. Let's say a thirty-five-year-old male non-smoker holds term insurance for thirty years and permanent insurance, like whole life or universal life, for thirty years as well. Below you can see the cost for term insurance added up over thirty years, compared to the cost of whole life over the same period, plus equity.

Age	Term 10 Life Insurance - $500,000		Universal Life Insurance - $500,000	
	Annual Premiums	Cash Value in Policy	Annual Premiums	Total Funds in Policy
35	$335.00	$0.00	$1,900.00	$1,729.00
36	$335.00	$0.00	$1,900.00	$3,533.00
37	$335.00	$0.00	$1,900.00	$5,451.00
38	$335.00	$0.00	$1,900.00	$7,398.00
39	$335.00	$0.00	$1,900.00	$9,467.00
40	$335.00	$0.00	$1,900.00	$11,632.00
41	$335.00	$0.00	$1,900.00	$13,897.00
42	$335.00	$0.00	$1,900.00	$16,266.00
43	$335.00	$0.00	$1,900.00	$18,741.00
44	$335.00	$0.00	$1,900.00	$21,327.00
45	$1,570.00	$0.00	$1,900.00	$24,028.00
46	$1,570.00	$0.00	$1,900.00	$26,846.00
47	$1,570.00	$0.00	$1,900.00	$29,786.00
48	$1,570.00	$0.00	$1,900.00	$32,851.00
49	$1,570.00	$0.00	$1,900.00	$36,046.00
50	$1,570.00	$0.00	$1,900.00	$39,374.00
51	$1,570.00	$0.00	$1,900.00	$42,843.00
52	$1,570.00	$0.00	$1,900.00	$46,459.00
53	$1,570.00	$0.00	$1,900.00	$50,226.00
54	$1,570.00	$0.00	$1,900.00	$52,194.00
55	$3,755.00	$0.00	$0.00	$54,225.00
56	$3,755.00	$0.00	$0.00	$56,314.00
57	$3,755.00	$0.00	$0.00	$58,459.00
58	$3,755.00	$0.00	$0.00	$60,658.00
59	$3,755.00	$0.00	$0.00	$62,907.00
60	$3,755.00	$0.00	$0.00	$65,202.00
61	$3,755.00	$0.00	$0.00	$67,539.00
62	$3,755.00	$0.00	$0.00	$69,911.00
63	$3,755.00	$0.00	$0.00	$72,312.00
64	$3,755.00	$0.00	$0.00	$74,735.00
65	$10,325.00	$0.00	$0.00	$77,169.00

Total Premiums Paid to Age 65:	$66,925.00	$38,000.00
Total Equity at Age 65:	$0.00	$77,169.00
Cost of Insurance at Age 65:	$66,925.00	Minus $39,169.00

*Note: Universal life policy does not require any premiums past age 55, but equity continues to grow, just like owning a house.

You can see that over a short period of time, term insurance is very cost-effective. It's a good way to cover short-term problems, like covering a debt. But if you use term insurance perpetually, it becomes much less efficient and more costly. Whole life and universal life, on the other hand, are the opposite. Let's go back to the renting versus owning analogy. Renting a home for a few years is a good way to give yourself shelter until you can move onto something better. But imagine if you rent for thirty years. All this time, you'll be paying more and more money, and when the time comes to move, you'll have nothing to show for it. Owning the home for thirty years, however, allows you to build equity. So, if you pay off the home and then sell it five years later, you have five years' worth of equity *and* you can recoup the money you put into the home in the first place. It's a very efficient way of buying a house, and permanent insurance is a very efficient way of buying insurance.

Once you know what your needs are, your planner can recommend the type that will best fulfill those needs. And like with investing, you'll know you have the right insurance if you can explain why you have it and what needs it's satisfying.

The Fine Print: Most life insurance policies—including disability, critical illness, and long-term care, for that matter—are underwritten by an insurance company through a licensed insurance agency. That is, a licensed insurance agent sits down with you and goes through the underwriting process to form a contract. The agent will ask you questions about your health, your lifestyle (such as whether you drink or smoke), your income, and so on. The agent then sends the information to the insurance company to verify if the information is correct. This is done to determine if you are insurable or not. If death is already knocking on your door, for example, no life insurance company will want to insure you. Insurance companies don't do business at the funeral home. By then it's already too late.

When the insurance company approves you, they will send you an actual insurance policy. This policy is a *contract*. More specifically, it's a *unilateral* contract. It binds the insurance company to pay the proceeds upon your death. There are usually two exclusions. One is called a suicide period. If you commit suicide within two years after receiving the contract, your policy typically becomes null and void. The other exclusion is called the incontestability period. If the insurance company finds out within the first two years that the information you gave was incorrect, then the terms of your policy will be adjusted accordingly. However, if the insurance company discovers at *any time* that the information you gave was *deliberately* fraudulent, as opposed to simply incorrect, your policy will typically be declared invalid.

Many companies will not issue life insurance to people who have pre-existing health conditions, like cancer. The reason is that insurance companies are hoping you live a long, healthy life. But if there's some condition you have that might prevent that, then forget it. To the insurance company, you're uninsurable. It's too big of a risk. (Sometimes the insurance company *may* reconsider after a waiting period of three to five years, but your financial planner will have to ask them if they will.)

This leads me to one of the most important facts about life insurance: the earlier you start, the better. How early am I talking about? I'm talking *very* early. Even childhood isn't too early.

Whenever I bring this up to my clients, the response is usually the same: "What? You want me to buy life insurance on my *child?*" They think it's morbid. They'll say, "I don't want to benefit from the death of my child."

But that's not the point. The reason it's smart to buy life insurance for your child is not so you can benefit, but because it's the *cheapest time in his or her life that that child can ever have life insurance.* The longer they live, the more they have to pay for it. But if you can buy it early, you can buy it cheap. Life insurance will always cost less for a twenty-five-year-old than a seventy-five-year-old because, again, insurance companies want you to live a long time. That's how they make money.

In fact, if you structure it properly, your child might never have to make a payment on his or her life insurance. Remember, with whole life insurance, you can pay it off ahead of time. When your child is twenty-five years old and getting married, he or she already has a good foundation.

In other words, the benefit for buying life insurance on your child is not for you. It's for your kid and *his or her* kids after that. So, think about it, Mom and Dad, or Grandma and Grandpa. Think what an enormous gift that is. Maybe they can't open it on Christmas morning, but I promise you: it'll mean more to them in the long run than any toy ever did. And again, the equity can be substantial and can be at their disposal when they get older, if you so choose. In other words, you control the equity until you feel they can make decisions on their own. In fact, life insurance can be used to cascade wealth to your heirs, sometimes without having to rely on an expensive trust for your child or grandchild.

Just so you know, I'm speaking from personal experience on this. This is what we did for my son. When he was fifteen days old, we bought life insurance for him. It cost peanuts. The reason is that I once had a client whose son became uninsurable when he was only fifteen years old. This young man will probably live a long and healthy life, but he'll never be able to buy life insurance due to a health condition. I didn't want that to happen to my kid, and I don't want it to happen to yours, either. By purchasing life insurance for your children, you're essentially protecting them. Once you buy life insurance, it can never be taken away. Even if you *become* uninsurable, it doesn't matter as long as you *already* purchased the life insurance. That's why I said that the best insurance is the insurance you have in place when you need it.

There are a lot of problems that life insurance can solve. Here is an example. Say you own a business and have two children. One child doesn't have any interest in running the business after you die, while the other does. If the company is valued at, say, $500,000, you can purchase a life insurance policy for an equal amount. The child who doesn't want to continue in the business can get the life insurance policy, while the other gets the business. This is estate equalization—both your heirs get a different part of your estate for equal value. However, this could possibly create a tax problem for the child taking over the company. So, what *that* child can do is purchase life insurance on *your* life, which he or she can then use to take care of any tax problems that might arise, if that child so chooses. Once again, this is all part of the planning process and is another reason for having an experienced financial planner.

UNDERWRITING AND GROUP INSURANCE

Underwriting occurs with all types of insurance, not just life. Whenever you receive an underwritten policy from an insurance company, it is always better than a policy that has not been underwritten, like with group insurance. That's because group insurance typically will not determine the validity of a claim until a claim is actually made. Be aware of this. Make sure that when you have group insurance, you always understand the claims process. Another thing to remember is that you don't *own* or *control* group insurance. Your employer controls it or your creditor controls it. Why is that important? If you ever stop working for that employer, you'll no longer have group insurance. That's why it's always a good idea to have some of both, as each can supplement the other. After all, your next employer might not offer group insurance. So, always have underwritten insurance to back it up.

With underwritten life insurance, you *know* your beneficiaries will receive a benefit after your death because the company has already determined you are insurable and have already gone over the exclusions. That's the underwriting process. They have agreed to pay the money.

If you purchase group insurance, usually through a creditor, you must remember that your policy will typically not be underwritten. In essence, the insurance company has not yet determined whether you are insurable or what exclusions may apply to you until *after* you die or become disabled. You'll be paying them money for a potential future benefit, but the details will be deliberately left grey. When insurance isn't underwritten, there's no way to know if you'll actually get the benefit or not. If you die and the company decides you weren't actually insurable when you bought the policy or that you violated one of the exclusions, it's possible your benefit won't be paid out.

If you have group insurance, you pay the premium *assuming* you're insured, but your family won't truly know until you actually die. That's when the insurance company will validate the claim. Obviously, this can lead to major problems.

The point of writing all this is to illustrate how important it is that your insurance be underwritten. It's something very few people know about or pay attention to, but it can end up being critical. Now, if group insurance is all you *can* get, take it. But don't count on it. If you have to take it, always ask what the exclusions are ahead of time. At the very least, you'll be more certain that you are truly insured.

THE FINANCIAL IMPLICATIONS OF INSURANCE

Hopefully it's a little bit clearer to you now how valuable insurance can be, and how it fits into your financial plan. That being said, I don't advocate everybody go out and just buy this stuff. And I certainly don't recommend that your planner sell it to you indiscriminately. Instead, he or she should perform an actual analysis of what your insurance needs are and the implications insurance will have on your finances.

A proper analysis of your situation can reveal one of two things about insurance: how much you need and how much you should get rid of. Yes, some people have too much insurance already, and any good financial planner will tell you that. If you have too much insurance, if some of it is overlapping, or the costs are outweighing the benefits, then you might consider getting rid of some of it. Keep in mind, though, that you may need it in the future, and if you're uninsurable, you may not be able to get it back. These are the kinds of situations you'll need to discuss with your planner.

I mentioned, too, that an analysis will show you the financial implications of whatever insurance you buy. For example, with long-term care insurance, we have to figure out how much it's going to cost. An analysis will help you with the following questions: "When am I going to need it?" and "What facility will I be going to?" and "How much will that cost?" It'll help you know what you'll need down the road and how you can offset the costs. You might have other assets you won't need once your long-term care begins, so if you don't need them, which ones can you use to help pay for LTC? An analysis can also show you how **Return of Premium** can create a more cost-effective, economically viable insurance program. More on this in a moment.

Or, take disability insurance. Suppose you buy disability insurance in your forties and then retire twenty-five years later at sixty-five. Let's say at that point that you don't need it anymore because you're retired. On the other hand, you paid for it all these years, and while it gave you peace of mind, you never actually had to use it.

Here's where your financial planner comes in. As long as the policy was structured properly, you could still get money back even though you are not disabled. You could still get a return on the premium. So, when I say "financial implications," I'm not only talking about the bad stuff. It could be good stuff, too.

To make disability and critical illness insurance more cost-effective and economically viable, you can buy it with a return of premium. What this means is you can recoup a percentage of your premium if you never make a claim. While insurance like this *does* cost more initially, it can end up returning money to you in the long run. For instance, say you buy disability insurance without return of premium. Assume it costs $30,000 between ages thirty and sixty-five. If you never filed a claim, by the time you retired, you would have spent a lot of money without any benefit other than peace of mind.

But with return of premium, the cost of your insurance would be $35,000 over the same period of time. However, you could get 75 percent of your premium returned to you if you don't make a claim. Seventy-five percent of $35,000 is $26,250, so the net cost of your disability insurance would only be $8,750. That's an absurdly small amount of money to pay to protect yourself from a potential accident.

The financial implications of dying are a little trickier. Here's an example. When you die, you trigger a new set of taxes called estate taxes in the United States and capital gains taxes in Canada, and your estate is required to pay that tax after you die. That's the responsibility of the executors and trustees. It would be a lot easier for them to pay that tax with insurance dollars rather than income dollars, right? And that's exactly what they can do with your life insurance money... again, providing you structure it right.

The point is, an analysis is key. Your financial planner will understand the value of insurance. Hopefully you do, too. But from his or her perspective, it shouldn't be just about selling it to you. From yours, it shouldn't be just about buying it. It should be about both parties coming together to understand exactly what insurance you need, how you'll pay for it, and how it'll affect the rest of your plan—your cash flow, taxes, funding agreements (like divorce agreements or buy-sell agreements), and so on.

Once you do that, you'll finally join the ranks of people who understand that insurance isn't an expense; it's an investment.

PLAN-GUARANTEE INSURANCE

Another reason insurance should be a part of your financial plan is that it also works as *plan-guarantee* insurance. Insurance can help guarantee your plan's security even if something unforeseen happens. And something unforeseen *will* happen. Don't ever let anyone tell you otherwise. Then there are the common problems you have to think about: you live too long, you die too soon, or you become disabled. Insurance helps protect your plan from all of those things.

Once upon a time, I sold some insurance to a dentist as part of his financial plan. While working on the plan, I met with his accountant. The accountant said our mutual client didn't need the insurance he bought because the things it covered would never happen to him. I asked the accountant what the alternative was, and he couldn't give me one. Then I asked him to give our client a written guarantee that he would never need the insurance, that bad things would never happen to him, and that if they did, the accountant would take care of him.

Obviously, that made the accountant stop and think.

If the accountant could have provided an alternative to insurance, I definitely would have considered it. I would never argue with a viable alternative, but the accountant couldn't provide one. When there is no viable alternative, that's when you turn to insurance. Once the accountant realized this, he conceded, and everything moved along according to the client's wishes.

Insurance is the only thing you can count on to protect you from the unexpected. Some people like to think they have other forms of protection, but what they don't realize is those other forms aren't guaranteed. I know a couple where the husband told his wife not to worry about buying insurance because he will take care of her if something ever happens. That's a great thing to say, on the surface. But what if something happens to him? What will happen to his wife if she needs to be cared for and he's no longer around? What about when he gets older and no longer has the same strength he has now? Again, can the husband *guarantee* that he can always take care of his wife?

No, he can't. But insurance *is* guaranteed. And that's why it's the only form of protection you can count on.

You've invested a lot of time and effort into your finances. You'll be investing time and effort into creating your financial plan very soon, and still more time and effort once the plan's in place. Don't put everything you've built at risk. Protect it. Don't let your plan become vulnerable. Pay a little more now so you don't have to pay everything later.

In my career, I hear a lot of people say, "I don't believe in insurance." I can never understand that comment. It's not a religion, so what is it you don't believe in?

Another thing I hear is, "I don't like insurance much." OK. But you can say the same thing about going to the doctor. Who actually likes going to the doctor? Or the dentist? Heck, you can say the same thing about not liking cops—most of us do say this whenever we get pulled over for speeding. But you still go to a doctor when you're sick or to a dentist when you've got a cavity. And you still call 911 whenever there's an emergency. So, saying you don't like something just isn't logical. You may not like it, but you still need it. It's still indispensable. That's true for doctors, and it's true for insurance.

The other common objection is, "I don't like insurance companies." But whenever insurance companies send cheques to people, *nobody* ever returns the cheque. No one ever has a problem with getting the money, and they are very happy they had the protection.

In the end, it's not that people don't believe in insurance or that they don't like it. They just don't want to pay for it. And that's not logical, either. Again, insurance is not an expense; it's a fail-safe, an investment. It's about protecting the things you value you most. It's about taking care of your loved ones. In the end, your loved ones are *always* worth paying for.

So, decide once and for all: Are you selfish or not? If your answer's the latter, then remember:

If you can't afford to lose it, then insure it.

KNOW YOU CAN

With a plan, you'll know how to make sure both you and your family are taken care of. Insurance is a big part of this. A plan will show you what types you need to protect yourself and your loved ones. It will also show you how to take advantage of the other benefits that come with insurance.

Insurance is yet another tool, another facet of your plan that you can use to solve problems. Everybody faces problems in this world, but not everybody knows if they can solve them. Having a financial plan means you know you can.

THIRTEEN

BUSINESS PLANNING

Pop quiz: Do you think Google, Apple, Microsoft, or Walmart got to where they are without a business plan?

The answer is NO. I promise you, they have a plan. Every successful company has a business plan. Sure, they might have all *started* with a single product or a single idea, but eventually things got to the point where they realized, "Hey, we want to make sure we do things right." Eventually they understood that there is more to running a successful business than just putting out a quality product.

So, they created a business plan.

A business plan is to a company what a regular financial plan is to an individual. It's the map that gets you to your destination, a checklist of everything you need to keep you in the air. It provides many of the same benefits as a regular financial plan, and it protects you from many of the same emergencies. That's because it solves problems instead of creating them.

In this chapter, we're going to talk a little bit about business planning.

Now, I understand this subject might not seem applicable to everyone. A lot of readers might not have their own business. But the principles apply no matter who you are. This chapter comprises two levels: first, we'll talk about the facets of business planning and how it applies to any of you entrepreneurs out there. Second, I'll show you how the principles of business planning also apply to regular individuals.

Every chapter in this book could have a whole book of its own devoted to it, and this one's no exception. It may seem overly simplistic to boil down a subject like business planning into a few short pages, but, like every chapter, this is meant to inspire you to go out and work with a professional planner to create a plan. It's meant to show you the benefits and solutions a plan can provide. So, with that said, let's delve into why *business* planning is so important.

It all starts with the "E-Myth."

Created by Michael Gerber in his book, *The E-Myth: Why Most Businesses Don't Work and What To Do About It,* the concept of the E-Myth started in the late '80s, The "E" stands for "entrepreneur," and it basically means that most people who start a business live in a fantasy world. They imagine they'll be rich and successful because they envision only the rewards of owning a business, not the risks.

"After all," they think, *"it worked for others, so why not me?"*

But the vast majority of businesses never get off the ground because the people who start them have no idea what they're getting into.

Now, that's not to say starting a business is *impossible*. I would never say that. But it's not *easy*. The E-Myth starts with the mind-set that everything is just going to fall into your lap. People will line up to come into your store, buy your product or your service, and then tell all their friends about it. All you have to do is show up to work.

At the heart of this myth is the fact that most business owners are really technicians, not entrepreneurs. For example, imagine a musician who opens a music store. A technician starts the business because she loves different instruments. She loves to spend her day talking about them, selling them, testing them, repairing them. So, that's exactly what she does. She works *in* the business. And that's fine, as far as it goes. It's even a little bit romantic. But when our music lover starts spending all day fixing instruments, she ignores the big-picture aspects of running a business. She ignores, for example,

- how to market;

- how to handle customer service issues;

- how to structure her business;

- how to recover in the event of a catastrophe, like if the economy plummets;

- how to expand the business; and

- how to fend off (or outmuscle) competitors.

And so on.

An entrepreneur, on the other hand, works *on* the business. Maybe she does *some* of the day-to-day work, but she spends most of her time working on the bullet points above. She's making the decisions that cause her business to grow.

Technicians don't really have a business to begin with. They have jobs. All they're doing is personally creating a product or providing a service, which is really no different than running a hot-dog stand or delivering newspapers. Entrepreneurs are the ones who have businesses instead of jobs because they're managing, not servicing. They're dealing with all the things that impact the success or failure of a business, such as taxes, insurance, marketing, expansion, competition, and local laws. But most people don't do that. They're technicians, not entrepreneurs. They have a job, not a business.

That's why most businesses fail. That's the E-Myth.

How is this analogous to everyday individuals? Most people have the same narrow perspective when it comes to their finances. Think of it like this:

Technicians don't manage their businesses; most people don't manage their finances. Think about everything we've talked about in this book so far. Take all the different aspects of the average person's finances. We know most people ignore them because most people don't have plans. They pay their taxes, but they don't know how to make their tax structure more efficient. They have investments, but they don't know if their investments are right for them or if they're on track to reach their goals because they don't have any. They haven't set up their estate, haven't purchased the right insurance, haven't paid attention to their expenses. They plan on retiring, but they haven't planned on how to pay for their retirement.

The same is true of most businesses. These businesses haven't done any tax planning, don't have proper insurance, haven't worked out what will happen in the event of an emergency. So, the E-Myth applies to individuals just as it applies to businesses. Most people work on making money, but they don't work on how to make their money work for them. They're not entrepreneurs of life; they're merely technicians.

Once people decide to become entrepreneurs and not technicians, the next step is to create a plan.

Sound familiar?

But remember what we talked about in the chapter on knowing if you've got a good plan? The temptation will always be there to do it yourself. That's true for individuals, and it's true for newly minted entrepreneurs. Either they're trying to save a buck or they think of themselves as do-it-yourselfers, selfishly forgetting about the consequences to other people if they get it wrong.

Yet, somehow, I don't think Steve Jobs, Bill Gates, or the McCain family were do-it-yourselfers when it came to their business plan.

I can't tell you how many people I've had come to me without the slightest idea of the basic fundamentals of business planning. Yet, they already have corporations—not just a business, but a corporation! For instance, once upon a time, a man named Brad came to see me. Brad had recently started a business, but he knew nothing about business planning. When I looked over his business, I said, "OK, Brad, you have a business, and that's great, but why did you set it up as a corporation?"

Now, I know the reason for having a corporation. Generally, there are two: limited liability and tax benefits. Limited liability means that if the corporation fails, they are not liable for the debts owed to their creditors. The shareholders of the corporation might lose their investments, and employees will lose their jobs, but in its simplest form, neither has to pay back any debts they owe.

The other advantage is that corporations are often taxed at a lower rate to promote the hiring of more employees.

Sounds great, right? But here's the problem: corporations aren't for everyone. They certainly weren't right for Brad. Brad didn't have much, if any, liability, and his corporation wasn't going to save him much in taxes because he didn't need to have many employees, at least to begin with. The little he saved in taxes wouldn't offset the amount it cost him to register his corporation in the first place or the headaches of managing a corporation. There's a lot more paperwork with a corporation, and a lot more reporting than if he'd just run his business as a sole proprietor. Ultimately, his corporation wasn't going to save him a lot of money, and it definitely wouldn't save him a lot of work.

Why did he choose to set up a corporation? Because his accountant told him to. If Brad had a proper business plan done by a proper planner, he would have known all this, but he decided to do it himself, and in the end took some really bad advice. His accountant probably recommended he go the corporate route because it would have been better for the accountant. The accountant wanted to be paid to set up corporate tax returns instead of just an individual tax return because, that way, he could charge more money. What his accountant *should* have said was, "Brad, you don't need to set up a corporation right now. What you need is a proper business plan." But there's no revenue for the accountant that way. So, he gave self-serving advice, and Brad, wanting to do it all himself, just decided to go along.

And that's what I usually see from new entrepreneurs. They come to me not knowing the first thing about business, thinking they can create their business plan all on their own. But ask yourself: Would you design your house on your own, even if you knew nothing about architecture?

Of course you wouldn't.

The first step in creating a successful business is to be an entrepreneur, not a technician. The same goes for individuals when it comes to their personal finances. The second step is to get a proper plan done, with the help of a competent professional who specializes in business planning. And, as we already know, that goes for individuals, too. In this day and age, finance has become so broad that it's pretty foolish to try to manage it all on your own. Most people just don't know enough. Or, if they do, they don't have the time. And even if they have the time, they probably don't have the will.

Until they meet with a planner.

Hopefully you're beginning to see why business planning is so important, and how it's analogous to personal financial planning. But let's take it a few steps further.

What is your business plan actually going to do for you?

Answer: the same sort of things your personal financial plan would.

Let's go through a quick checklist of the items your financial plan will cover:

1. Tax planning

2. Cash flow

3. Insurance needs

4. Your will

5. Investments

The checklist for your business plan should look almost identical. For example:

TAX PLANNING

We've already covered how tax planning is not the same thing as tax preparation. Tax preparation just involves paying the taxes you already owe, with your accountant functioning as a scorekeeper between you and the Canada Revenue Agency (or IRS if you're in the United States). *Planning* involves predicting the taxes you'll owe *in the future* and then making the necessary adjustments to bring that number down. Since you want to keep as much of your money as legally possible, tax planning is a vital part of managing your finances.

It's no different for a business. Many new business owners and their accountants focus only on tax preparation. But what about the taxes you'll owe next year? And the year after that? What happens if you decide to expand or hire more employees or move to a new location? The taxes you owe could be dramatically different. Take Brad and his corporation. What if he set up his business as a corporation but then realized it wasn't a good idea? For example, imagine that Brad had a loss in his first year of operation. If he had a corporation, he wouldn't have anything to write his losses off against because he hadn't paid any corporate income taxes yet. He could carry those losses *forwards*, but he couldn't carry them back. On the other hand, if he had a proprietorship, he *could* write his losses off against the tax returns he'd filed as an individual in previous years. So, if at any point Brad decided he didn't want to be a corporation, he would have to restructure. But restructuring would have an effect on Brad's taxes, too. Suddenly, next year rolls around, and since Brad's situation is much different from when he started, he might find himself owing a *lot* more in taxes than he anticipated—more, in fact, than he could actually pay.

We've got a word for what happens next: *bankruptcy*.

Every business plan should have tax planning involved. It's vital for individuals, and it's vital for businesses.

CASH FLOW

Your cash flow is how much money you have coming in and how much you have going out. When my company, HSI Financial Group, does financial plans for individuals, calculating a client's cash flow is part of how we determine whether they need to save more, earn more, or invest more money in order for them to meet their financial goals.

As you can imagine, it's absolutely *critical* that businesses track their cash flow. A business has to have a positive cash flow, or it will not remain solvent for long. Cash flow allows businesses to track how much money they are making, how much it is costing them to produce their goods or deliver their services, and how much money is being allocated to overhead, such as payroll, taxes, insurance, marketing, rent, and utilities. As with an individual, if a business's cash flow isn't good, a business plan can recommend how to change that—or, at least, what areas need to be changed. And if your cash flow is positive, then you can determine how much money you have to reinvest in the business, which will help improve the net worth of your company, and that is the real yardstick for success.

To ignore your cash flow is like ignoring what you eat. People who do that have too many calories coming in and not enough going out or vice versa. When you're underweight or overweight, you leave yourself vulnerable to a whole world of health problems.

It's the same for your finances. Businesses aren't immune. Neither are regular people. To watch your financial diet, you have to track your cash flow. To do that, you need a plan.

INSURANCE NEEDS

As previously mentioned, insurance is your financial safety net. It's your second engine. It's what keeps your plan going, even when turbulence hits.

And for businesses? Insurance is what can keep your business going, even when disaster strikes. But many business owners have no idea what insurance they need. In fact, I've even come across people who think their personal insurance will protect them from any liability. But your insurance may not protect you if your delivery truck crashes into a parked car or if someone sues you because they burned their tongue on the coffee you serve.

There are all sorts of situations in a person's life that can be covered by insurance. Maybe you'll need them; maybe you won't. But there are just as many things that could happen to your business. If your business is your livelihood, do you really want to leave it unprotected?

No, you don't. Remember: if you can't afford to lose it, then insure it.

YOUR (BUSINESS) WILL

With businesses, I also see the absence of a buy-sell agreement. A buy-sell agreement, also known as a USA or Unanimous Shareholder's Agreement, can be thought of as a will for your business.

In your personal life, we talked about how it's so important to decide what will happen to your estate after you die or who can make decisions for you if you get sick. These things have to be done for businesses, too. For example, say you have a partner, but at some point your partner becomes disabled and can't work anymore. What happens to his side of the business?

Well, two things can happen. For those businesses without a buy-sell agreement, the healthy partner ends up having to do twice the work for the same amount of money. That would be you. Meanwhile, the partner who *can't* work sends the spouse to take over his or her side of the business. But maybe you don't like your partner's spouse. Or maybe the spouse just has no real interest or competency in the business you're running. So, now you're saddled with more work *and* a lot of dead weight to deal with. That kind of thing can make a business tank really fast.

Businesses that *do* have a buy-sell agreement can deal with this kind of scenario much more easily. With a buy-sell agreement, you've already worked out what happens in advance. If your partner can't work anymore, you will already have an arrangement in place to buy out his or her share of the company—hence, the term "buy-sell." One partner buys; the other sells. You could even have it structured so that your insurance pays for your partner's half of the business.

As a business owner, you also have to determine what will happen to your business after you die. Who will it go to? If you're in a partnership, a buy-sell agreement will determine who your partner agrees to work with after you're gone, and vice versa. The buy-sell agreement could stipulate that your oldest son becomes the new partner or that an outsider can buy your family's side of the business.

Buy-sell agreements are particularly important when a married couple owns a business together. Unfortunately, in these situations such agreements are most neglected. But they shouldn't be. What if you and your spouse get divorced? The end of a marriage shouldn't necessarily spell the end of your business, but it could without a buy-sell agreement.

Quick note: there are three more agreements couples should consider, whether they have a business or not. The first is a pre-nuptial agreement, which couples should think about before they get married. The second is a marriage agreement, for couples who are already married. The third is a cohabitation agreement for couples living in a common-law relationship. These agreements are often neglected as well, but they really need to be discussed with your planner. This topic is beyond the scope of this book, so I won't say anymore here. But to make a long story short, these agreements are important. Don't overlook them.

When arranging a buy-sell agreement, decide how to fund it. How exactly will one partner buy out the other if it ever becomes necessary? Here again is another example of why working with a planner is so important. A planner can show you the different options available and can even link different parts of your plan together. For instance, your plan should provide not only for your insurance needs and your buy-sell agreement; it should also link the two together. Business Plan Guarantee Insurance can help you if your partner becomes disabled or passes away. It can also fund a buy-sell arrangement if you can't pay for it all yourself. Typically, insurance is the cheapest way to fund a buy-sell, but many business owners don't know that—unless they work with a planner.

Regardless of how it's structured, how you pay for it, or who your partner is, a buy-sell agreement is one of the most fundamental aspects of owning a business. It drives me nuts when businesses don't have one. Do they honestly think that nothing bad will ever happen, such as a partner retiring or dying? Or that these things will just take care of themselves? Read the business section of a newspaper sometime and keep an eye out for headlines about companies going under. If you read about a business where the founder died, and her kids are all squabbling over what to do with the company, then you can bet they never had a buy-sell agreement. Many a proud company has met their end that way.

KNOW YOU CAN

There's one more reason why business planning is so important.

After you finish this book, I hope the first thing you do is look for a planner to work with, someone to help get your personal finances in order. But when you find your planner, keep this in mind:

Your business plan is a part of your personal financial plan.

Remember this because it's the main reason I wrote this chapter. It would be a major mistake to think of your business plan and your financial plan as being separate. They're not. Your financial plan should encompass *all* of your finances in life, and that includes your income. So, if your business is your income, don't you think your business should be a part of your financial plan?

The best way to include it is to have a business plan, which will ensure you always have a business to plan for. Think of your business plan as being a subsection of your overall financial plan. It's no less important a piece than anything else.

That's true of the rest of your plan, too. No one piece is less important than another because even a small piece can change your life. If you take out a single piece from a jigsaw puzzle, the picture is ruined. The piece you take out might seem insignificant, but the puzzle would be unfinished without it. If you take away a piece of equipment from an airplane, even if it's tiny, you might not be able to get off the ground. Regardless of size, the piece is a part of the whole. The rest of the airplane depends on that piece. So does the picture in your jigsaw puzzle. And so does your financial plan. People who know their finances inside and out, who pay attention to *every* piece, are the ones who often have the most success in life.

Actually, that's why pilots always do a walk-around before flying their airplane. A walk-around is exactly what it sounds like: the pilot walks around the craft, inspecting it for any problems. It's not something that should be taken lightly. You'll never see expert pilots conduct a lazy walk-around. They know their plane inside and out, and they understand the value of even the smallest pieces.

Once, when I was doing a walk-around, I noticed a white, plastic zip tie near my landing gear. It wasn't easy to spot because my plane is white, too. But I was taking care with my walk-around, so I spotted it. The zip tie was designed to hold some wires together, but a few were loose. If I had taken off with my plane like that, the landing gear would have come up and rubbed against the wires. Those wires are important; they're indicator wires, letting me know when my gear is down so I can land, among other things. If something were to happen to them, it could be a big problem.

I called a mechanic and said, "Take a look at this. I'm a little concerned about it. Can we reach in there and strap another tie around those wires?"

"Sure we can," the mechanic said, "but you know, I'm impressed you caught that because it's not easy to spot."

I appreciated the compliment, but at the same time it was a rather funny thing to say. How could you *not* notice it, unless you were doing a real lazy walk-around? That's what a walk-around is *for*, to catch things like that, to spot a missing screw or a loose rivet. These might be small pieces, but they're still important because they're connected to the rest of the plane. Everything is interconnected in a plane, and the same is true for your financial plan. *Everything is connected.* No piece is more important than the other. They're all critical.

So, when you meet with your planner, make sure you take your business plan along. Or, if you don't have one yet, ask your planner to help you with it. Then get it done because your plan will only work if *everything* goes into it.

Owning a business can be very difficult and very complex. As a business owner myself, I can personally attest to this. But you don't have to do it alone. Your financial planner will be your co-pilot when it comes to properly setting up a business. Just as pilots depend on their co-pilot to help them with all the intricacies of flying a plane, so too should you depend on *your* co-pilot to help with all the intricacies of owning a business. Owning a business is a tricky matter, but with the help of a financial plan, you'll always know that you can.

By the way, if you're still on the fence about the need for a plan, think of it like this: a successful business always has a plan. Sony, Apple, Walmart, and Target have plans. The most prosperous entrepreneurial minds in the world all have plans.

Shouldn't you have one, too?

FOURTEEN

FINANCIAL HARMONY IN THE HOME

We're getting very near to the end of the book. But before we wrap up, it's time to look at one of the most important effects of having a financial plan: harmony in the home.

When couples get married or decide to live together, they almost always dream of a future where they are happy, affluent, and in love (not necessarily in that order). Whether their dream is having a white picket fence, traveling the world in a motor home, or spending their nights in sleeping bags under the stars, they all envision some kind of Happily Ever After. No one foresees themselves bickering over money. No one (except maybe rich, cynical celebrities) foresees getting separated or divorced. No one pictures living in a home that is anything less than harmonious.

Unfortunately, even Happily Ever Afters are punctuated by fights, disagreements, and bad feelings. In previous chapters, I've tried to show that experiencing misfortune isn't a matter of *if*, but *when*. It's inevitable. You *will* run into turbulence during your life. A big part of getting through it is by accepting that it will happen, and *planning* for it.

Turbulence often happens in the home, too, and like life in general, it's usually a matter of *when*, not *if*. It's hard to maintain harmony in the middle of strong turbulence, and couples who can't are usually the ones who end up separating. But, like life in general, turbulence doesn't have to be a disaster. It doesn't have to lead to divorce or even dislike. You can overcome it, especially if you plan for it.

By now you should see how having a financial plan can help protect you from so many bad things, or can at least make them easier to deal with. One of the great things about a financial plan is that it can help you *inside* the home as well as outside it. When a husband and wife, for example, create and follow a financial plan, it can do so much to maintain harmony in their relationship. I'll give a few examples below, but first, let's ask the inevitable question: What do finances have to do with harmony?

Financial issues are the leading cause of divorce in North America—not just in Canada, not just in the United States, but in all of North America. The reason is that financial issues put so much pressure on a couple. Now, there could always be other, deeper underlying issues to a couple's problems, but in either case, finances are what often breaks the camel's back. The wife spends too much. The husband spends too much. The husband's a cheapskate. The wife's a miser. Neither one will admit being the problem. Or, maybe it has nothing to do with spending. Maybe the husband doesn't make enough money, and it forces the wife to work when she'd rather stay home. Maybe the wife has health issues, and all their money has to go towards medical bills. Maybe they have different goals with what they want to do with their money. It could be anything. But because money is at the core of so much of daily life, it's hard to be happy if you're always worrying about it. And it's hard to be happy with *each other*. That means it's almost impossible to have harmony in the home.

A financial plan can help with many of these issues. As you've already seen, it can help determine what your goals are and what it will take to achieve them. It will help show what areas of your finances need work. It can also show you how much to earn, how much to save, how much to spend, how to minimize taxes, how to maximize your investments, how to protect yourself from financial catastrophes—you name it. The more issues your plan helps resolve, the less pressure is placed upon you and your family.

Notice, though, that I said a financial plan helps *maintain* harmony in the home, but it can't create it. That's because a plan can't do anything for what isn't there to begin with. A plan helps you determine the direction in which *everyone* wants to go. So, it can help you *find* consensus, but it can't help you create it.

Furthermore, financial planners aren't psychiatrists. They're not family counselors. They fix financial issues, not family issues. If there's no harmony in the home to begin with, chances are you won't be coming in to create a financial plan in the first place. If you do, you won't actually follow it (probably because it won't represent both of you, or one of you didn't want to be there).

That's what I sometimes see, actually, when couples come to see me. I can usually tell pretty quickly which couples have harmony in the home and which don't. For the latter, it's usually because one spouse dominates the relationship. Maybe she's abusive; maybe he's a control freak; maybe she's dismissive of her spouse's thoughts and feelings. At the end of the day, the toughest situations are when it's the man who dominates. Usually, he thinks he knows everything, that everything is cool as long as his wife conforms to what he wants. It's pretty hard to have harmony in cases like that, and all but impossible to create an *accurate* financial plan. Now, when I see couples like that, I can certainly talk to them about it, but I can't fix it. They have to be the one who's willing to say, "You know what? You're right."

Early in my career, I used to make a lot of house calls. One night I had an appointment in a couple's home. When I arrived, I found the husband watching hockey, even though we had a meeting scheduled. Now, I like hockey as much as the next person, but I was there for business, and I believe in keeping my appointments. You would think the game could wait, right?

Not to this guy. I had to wait until the end. His wife kept me company, but I could tell she was angry. You could see it on her face. Yet, she never said a thing; she just put up with it. He was in charge, and she had to wait on him. So, she put the kids to bed, which gave us a little bit of time, but otherwise we both had to wait for him to shut off the TV.

When he finally did, we sat down and I explained some things. She listened closely, but it was clear her husband couldn't care less. You could tell. He just wandered all over the place, distracted. It was very rude.

Still, we put the basics of a plan together. We looked at their financial situation. They—or rather, the wife—decided to purchase life insurance because they had absolutely no life insurance whatsoever. The husband wasn't happy. Even though he had two young children, this wasn't the way he wanted to spend their money. But the wife wanted to, so he went along with it, probably just to get me out of there.

The next week, the husband called me up. I had almost everything ready. Their plan was written, their investments ready to go, their savings programs in place. But when I answered the phone, he said, "You know that life insurance that we set up last week, and those investments? Go ahead and cancel all that now."

I said, "Oh, really? Why? What's the problem?"

He couldn't really give me a straight answer, so I finally said, "All right, should I cancel the automobile insurance, too?" (This was back when I also sold automobile insurance. It was a long time ago.)

"No, no, keep that," he said. "Just cancel the other stuff. I was just doing that to make my wife feel good."

Nice, right? Forget about harmony in the home. You can't have harmony when one person dominates the other or makes all the decisions. And, as the husband proved, you can forget about having a financial plan. But there was nothing I could do, so I said, "Consider it canceled. It's done."

A few months later, he gave me another call. "Wes, can you put the glass coverage on my car insurance?" In some parts of Canada, you can delete glass coverage on your automobile because it's a very expensive part of insurance. People's windshields get broken all the time, and it costs the insurance company a lot of money to replace them. You can delete the glass coverage off your car, which keeps your premium down but makes you responsible for your own windshield. As you can guess, the husband didn't want to pay the extra money at first. But now he suddenly wanted to add coverage.

I said, "Why? Did you break your window?"

"Yeah."

"Sorry, buddy," I replied. "It doesn't work that way. See, when you're dead in the grave, I can't sell you life insurance, either."

He grunted, groaned, and went away, but it wasn't long until he actually came into my office. Now he wanted to talk about life insurance. I asked him, "Why the change of heart?" But he didn't even have to answer. I knew what was going on. It was almost certainly family trouble. So, it came as no surprise when he said, "She's leaving me."

"So, you think insurance is going to fix that?" I asked. "It's probably too little, too late. Besides, I really don't want to do business with you. Your heart's not in it." (Remember, part of picking a financial planner means you have to feel comfortable with that person. If you don't feel comfortable with the planner or the planner doesn't feel comfortable with you, that's a sign it's not going to work.)

He went away and got divorced, but there's a happy ending to this story; his ex-wife became a client of mine. Twenty-eight years later, she's still a client and doing great.

If you're a jerk, neither I nor any financial planner can turn you into a nice guy. If you're a jerk or a control freak, there probably won't be any harmony in your home. The same is true if you've got the opposite problem: if you're timid or passive and let your spouse do all the work. You really need to know about these things ahead of time because at the end of the day, most of us can think of at least one communication issue in our home that revolves around money. Most problems in the home get around to money eventually because even if your finances aren't the root of the issue, they will definitely exacerbate it. Those issues have to be settled—or at least acknowledged—before you start trying to create a plan.

When you think about it, how much more harmony could people bring to their lives if they communicated better with their spouse, if they were on equal footing? How much easier would life be? How much tension and stress would you take off your family if you could have that conversation?

Where a planner *can* help is with that conversation. Planners can help coach you and your family in communicating, as long as everyone agrees they need help with it. At HSI, we can sit down with Mom, Dad, or even the kids. We'll offer to sit down and have a conversation with them about money matters, to explain to them what's going on and how they can contribute. If Dad's going through a lot of stress because of his job, maybe he doesn't want to share things with the rest of the family. Maybe he doesn't want to tell them, "Kids, there's certain things we can't afford right now." Well, if he doesn't want to tell them, we can.

Some people will say, "Oh, I don't want the kids to worry about that." Well, when are the kids going to learn, then, if we don't have that conversation? How will they deal with it when *they're* married? Probably the same way as their parents, so the cycle just begins again.

Here's what I'm saying: harmony in the home comes down to communication—not panicking, not screaming, not keeping things to yourself, not doing everything *by* yourself. I can say this with complete confidence because it's not just Wes Forster the Financial Planner saying it; it's Wes Forster the person. I grew up in a home without much financial harmony. There was too little communication taking place, which could have solved many of our family's financial issues with a lot less stress and headaches.

Now, all of this isn't to say that things have to be *perfect* at home before you go see a financial planner. Far from it. The point is that you have to know if there *is* a problem. Both halves of a couple have to be on equal footing and on common ground. Both have to acknowledge their mutual strengths and weaknesses. Both need to have common goals and a common desire to reach those goals. As long as *that's* done, there can at least be financial harmony in the home. That's what harmony *is*. And if there's harmony, having a financial plan will enable you to take it to the next level.

In short, you need to have that communication in place before you go see a financial planner. Or, you need to have the *willingness* and *desire* to have that communication. As long as both people are engaged with the process, your financial planner can help you overcome the rest. But if one person is never engaged at all and doesn't care, it will be very, very difficult. If you came in to see me, we could still have the conversation, and I could point out what I'm saying now, but nothing else could happen until the light bulb clicked on and both parties agreed to make a change.

One couple I worked with exemplifies this idea perfectly. We'll call them Ned and Alice. Ned was wealthy but frugal—a very organized man and a very smart man. He liked to be in control. Alice, on the other hand, was more passive, a bit more carefree. So, as you can imagine, it was Ned who managed the money.

When Ned came to us, he wanted his finances to be organized and planned for just like everything else. He was getting older and didn't want to be dealing with so many details anymore. He wanted to enjoy life. But the thing with Ned is that he never wanted to spend any money. I had to work to get him to *spend* money; usually it's the opposite.

Because Alice had a different personality and because he controlled their finances, he was always concerned that she would get crazy and go on some big spending spree. It's a very common feeling that controlling people have about their partners when there's not enough communication taking place. Ned expressed that fear to me. Alice's complaint was different. "He's so cheap," she told me once. "He doesn't want to spend any money." So, each had this different viewpoint, but since they didn't really communicate well about it, they both just ended up being frustrated.

But the good thing about Ned and Alice is that they really loved each other. When they came in to see me, they both wanted to be there. They both, I think, wanted to make a change. They had different personalities, but those differences didn't drive them apart. Part of the planning process was helping them communicate better with each other so that each could understand what the other wanted. And because they both had the *desire* and the *ability* to improve their communication, it worked.

As it turns out, Alice didn't want to just go and spend a bunch of money on herself. She just wanted to use their money to do things *together*, to improve both their lives. For example, when Ned first came to me, he drove this old minivan. That thing was a menace on the road. It was a death trap. So, she wanted him to buy a new car for *himself*. She would say, "Why don't you go out and buy yourself a new car? You've worked hard. You deserve it."

I don't know about you, but I think that's a pretty nice thing for a spouse to say.

He finally admitted that he wanted a Lincoln. But part of his concern, I think, was that he felt if he bought himself a car, he'd have to buy her one, too. But she just wanted him to loosen up a little bit and get what he wanted so that he'd be happier. So, I did the plan and showed him the numbers. I said, "You know, you really *can* afford this. Here's how we can make this happen." And we made it happen. He got himself that Lincoln, and he enjoyed the heck out of it.

A bit later he came in again, and this time he was a lot more comfortable. He understood where his wife was coming from. It made them both feel better. Because we had talked about it together, and because he was willing to listen, we were able to make this great plan that got him what he wanted. So, when he came in again, he was a bit more comfortable with the idea of spending money. I told him that this was what planning was all about. I said, "You know, it's OK for you to spend your money if you have it. And you *do* have it. That's why you came to see me in the first place, to see how much money you could spend, to see what it would take to retire and all that. If you follow the plan, you won't run out of money. So, I have to agree with Alice. Why don't you go enjoy yourself a little bit? Why else have you worked so doggone hard? To lay there dying in bed, knowing you have a lot of money that you never bothered to enjoy with your wife and grandchildren?"

He nodded. He was coming around. I said, "Let me reiterate. If I think you're spending too much money or that your wife is spending too much, I'll tell you. That's what I'm here for."

Then he started to share with me the things he thought his *wife* wanted. I said, "And you think you can't afford all this, right?"

"Well, no," he replied. "Actually, I'm beginning to see we *can* afford it." (Notice he used the word "we.")

"It might surprise you to find out, Ned," I told him, "that your wife really isn't the spendthrift you thought she was." He agreed. Even though they'd been married for forty years or so, he was just realizing this—because they were finally able to communicate about it.

"So," I said, "we've helped get you what you want. Do you know what *she* wants? Because that's the next step. Why don't you go learn what she wants, and then we'll have a meeting to find out if you can do it or not."

We had that meeting not too long afterwards. I said to Alice, "OK, so what is it you want to do? What are *your* goals?" She started explaining them to me, and the whole time I'm keeping an eye on Ned. He didn't say anything. He just listened, clearly comfortable with it. Ned was a really nice man, but now he was starting to become a more open and trusting man as well. Instead of only paying attention to *his* concerns, he was letting her speak for the both of them.

After we went through the list, we crunched some numbers and set up a budget. He looked at it and just lit up. "Oh, that's not so bad." He was happy because his biggest concerns were being met, and she was happy because her goals were being reached. And Ned even started getting excited when he realized he could help her with some of her goals, and that it would be fun for both of them.

She also wanted to make some changes in her own life. I said, "OK, so what you have to do, Alice, is put a list together. What do *you* want? Give me the list, we'll research the cost, and then we'll get the wheels rolling." This was about four years ago. I never saw the list. She never got it to me, but she was as happy as can be. Why was she happy? Because she knew that if she *wanted* to make changes, she could do it. She knew her husband would support her. And that's important in a marriage—the knowledge that your spouse supports you in whatever you do.

Ned has since passed away, but he's left some very good memories for Alice and his family to treasure every day. They truly were a couple that achieved financial harmony in their home.

How do you change the way you communicate if a change is necessary? It starts with being willing to admit your part in creating harmony in the home. It starts with saying, "I am partners with my spouse. I love this person. I care about this person. I love my family. I genuinely care about providing for them. I genuinely care about not being selfish." Or, if your spouse is the controlling person and *you're* the one being controlled, it starts with saying, "I am partners with my spouse. I deserve to have a say in what happens to our family. I care about what happens to us. I genuinely want to contribute." It starts with both partners saying, "Nothing is mine. Everything is *ours*," including both your family's finances *and* your family's future.

Remember, Ned's big fear was that Alice was going to spend all this money without regard to the consequences. But they never communicated with each other about it, so he always put his foot down on a non-existent issue. He was controlling her because he didn't trust her. And not trusting her was a terrible message to send. But when they came to see me, he realized he had to start communicating better. He realized that she deserved a say, too. That realization was the key. It was the key to both of them realizing their dreams. It was the key to creating a financial plan, the key to maintaining harmony in their home.

The key to having their own Happily Ever After.

KNOW YOU CAN

An important part of having harmony in the home is showing your family that you love them. What better way, what deeper way is there to demonstrate love than by showing them that you appreciate their needs? That you want to help them accomplish their goals? That you want them to be taken care of after you're gone? None that I know.

Everyone dreams of a Happily Ever After. A financial plan can't get that for you, but here's what it *can* do. The process of creating a financial plan can help you and your family work towards what you all want to accomplish. It can take away the doubt, the pressure, and the strain that comes from financial problems. And it can teach the value of communication.

So, will you and your family find your own Happily Ever After? I don't know. What I do know is that with a financial plan, you can go a long way to *securing* that happy ending. And once you have your plan, you'll know you can, too.

FIFTEEN

WHERE DO WE GO FROM HERE?

So now we've come to the end of the book. After reading about the benefits of having a financial plan, the dangers of procrastination, the ins and outs of what goes into a plan, and how to choose a planner, you're about to turn the last page. You're about to shut the back cover. Hopefully, you'll take a deep breath, set the book down, and lean back in your chair. If I've done my job, then you'll have come to realize just how crucial it is to have a financial plan, and what's more, why you should have one sooner rather than later. If that's the case, the inevitable thought going through your mind will be

"Where do I go from here?"

Fortunately, you'll already know the answer.

After you finish this book, the first step is to get serious about having a plan. Getting serious means you start without delay. Don't let a day or a week go by. Start now. (Or, if it's nighttime, start tomorrow morning.) If you do that, and if you follow the four steps I've written out below, then in ninety days—only ninety—you'll have taken control of your financial life. You'll have a plan in place that helps secure all the things you value: a plan that helps you achieve your goals and a plan that protects you and your family from the twists, turns, and sudden drops the future might have in store.

Where do you go from here? You embark on a ninety-day journey to change your financial life.

STEP ONE: KNOW YOUR MISSION

A few years ago, when I bought my airplane, I researched the heck out of it and learned as much as I could about which craft would be best for me. But the only way to find out was to first ask myself the following questions: "What mission is my airplane supposed to fly? What am I going to use it for? Will I fly rescue missions in it? If so, a medevac plane is the one for me. Do I want an airplane just for personal use, to take my family on vacation? Do I want to go sightseeing in my airplane? Do I want to land on water? Or, do I want to travel long distances and bring lots of passengers along for the ride? What part of the world will I be flying in?" These are the things you have to consider. In other words, "What's my mission?"

When it comes to your financial plan, the same question applies. Before you begin your journey, you have to know what your mission is. You have to decide what exactly you want your plan to do for you. What problems are you trying to solve? What objectives are you trying to meet? What fears are you trying to conquer?

Most people do a lot of things right when it comes to financial planning, long before they ever get a plan. But they may not do things in the right order, or they spend far too much time focused on one thing, to the detriment of everything else. The same was true of me when I bought my plane. Like I said, I did all my research. I knew what to look for and what to avoid because I consulted with experts beforehand. In fact, I paid them to help me so that I wouldn't make any expensive mistakes. After working with these experts, I knew how to tell if a plane was safe, if it would perform well, if it was mechanically sound. I knew that whatever I bought, it would be an excellent machine. That didn't mean, however, that I was immune to making a big mistake. I could have bought a plane that was way too big for the job. It would have been a waste of money and maintenance. The plane would have cost me more than what it's worth to do what I wanted it to do.

For example, I could have bought a 737 for sightseeing. That's a pretty expensive way to go sightseeing, unless I planned on traveling the length of the world. And even then, I wouldn't have been doing much sightseeing because I'd have been flying too high to see anything I really wanted to see. It still would have been a great airplane, but it wouldn't have been a great airplane for me. With a financial plan, the same thing applies. What exactly are you trying to accomplish? What's realistic for you? Do you want a plan that will help you create the time and money to go on vacation? Do you want a plan to help you get out of debt? To help you retire? To help you start your own business? Or a mixture of all these things and more? Answering these questions is the first step of the planning process. You have to know where you want to go before you set out to get there. Hopefully by now you know that you *can* get there, with the help of your plan.

Almost as important as knowing your mission is not allowing yourself to become fixated on one specific part of it. As I said above, don't get too focused on one thing to the detriment of everything else. For instance, let's say a part of your mission is to get your house paid off very quickly. It's really important to you that you have no debt. That's a great attitude to have and a great piece of a financial plan. There's no question about that.

But there are other pieces involved. You have to start thinking about education for your kids. And, of course, you want to retire at some point. Plus, you want to take a few vacations here and there, too. But your primary mission is to pay off your house, and when that's taken care of, and you've gone on a few vacations and helped your kids go to school, *then* you'll start thinking about saving for retirement. Retirement is just the farthest thing from your mind right now because the house comes first.

That's an example of fixating on one thing, and it's the biggest problem I see with younger people. They want to get the house paid off as soon as possible so they can start putting money towards other things. So, they pay it down and pay it down and push everything else to the side. When they pay the house off, they're only fifty and have no debt, but they have no savings, either. Going on vacation is out of the question, at least for a while, and suddenly they're looking ahead and retirement is only fifteen, twenty years away, and they haven't even started saving for it yet. What's more, they've barely given it any thought, so they have no idea how much they'll actually need.

In flying, allowing yourself to become fixated on one thing can be disastrous. In fact, it's the most dangerous thing that can happen to a pilot. If you're hand-flying a plane—as opposed to putting it on autopilot—through the clouds or through bumpy weather, you have to constantly check your instruments. Not just one instrument, but *all* your instruments. If you get fixated on one instrument or one problem, that's very, very dangerous. This is where a number of accidents have occurred in aviation.

Don't allow yourself to become fixated. It could be the demise of your financial plan. When you sit down to determine your mission, remember to consider *every* aspect of it. That way, when you actually get down to working with a planner, your plan will encompass your entire mission and not just one part of it. It'll help you reach all your goals and, what's more, put your goals in the right order.

So, your first step is to figure out your mission. Your second step is to find someone who can help you accomplish it.

STEP TWO: GO OUT AND FIND YOUR PLANNER

Time: thirty days

We've talked about this step quite a bit already, but here are just a few final words on the subject. How do you find your planner? My advice boils down to this:

Find the names of three planners in your area. Make sure it's at least three. Ask your friends and family if they're using a planner they're happy with. Don't rely *solely* on the recommendations your sister or your buddy down the street gives you. Remember, just because you're close to them doesn't mean you can trust their judgment. But you should definitely start by asking. Next, get on Google. Search for financial planners in your area. In Canada you can also get names from Advocis, a financial regulatory agency, or through the Financial Planners Standards Council. But really, all you need is Google. (Keep in mind, though, that just because a name is listed on Google's first page doesn't mean he or she is necessarily the best. It might just mean they have a really good website.) Once you've found three, go visit them. Compare them with each other. Ask them to read this book. But be careful about making one of those three your brother-in-law or old college roommate or someone like that. That could be a dangerous choice. How do you fire him or her if it doesn't work out?

When you start meeting with the three planners you've found, make sure they're accredited and have substantial experience. But again, don't rely on that alone. Just because someone has experience doesn't mean they're good. They could be at it for thirty years, but maybe they're doing the same things now that they were doing thirty years ago. Maybe they're not innovative. Experience is important, but it's not definitive. It's really important to remember that.

What's more definitive is this: Do they speak your language? Do they make you comfortable? (This point is crucial. If you're not comfortable with him or her in the first meeting, you probably won't be comfortable with that person later.) Ask to see a sample plan. Find out what your plan will look like when it's done. Find out how much it'll cost you. Find out how your planner is getting compensated. Remember, it's not important whether your planners charge fees or commissions or whatever, only that they're open and honest about it, and that they don't spend time bashing the opposite of whatever they do.

Choose a planner who makes you feel comfortable—because the sample plan covers all the bases we've talked about in this book, because the planner will help you work towards your vision, and because he values the same things you value. Don't be motivated by returns. Returns are temporary, never permanent. And remember to watch out for all the common hooks. The promise of great returns, for example, is a hook. Your planner saying, "Choose me because I never charge commissions" is a hook. (How, then, does he get paid?) The promise of lower taxes is a *huge* hook as well. If he says, "I'm going to save you all this money in taxes," then you *know* he is trying to hook you. How can he possibly know if he'll save you taxes when he hasn't even created your plan yet?

References are useful, as long as you remember that the planner is only giving you access to her very best clients. What I do when I provide references is I try to match up the reference with the person I'm meeting with. I try to choose a reference who has a similar temperament, goals, and financial situation. Maybe he's the same age; maybe he's in the same profession. That kind of reference is a lot more helpful for prospective clients. Ask your planner if she can do the same for you.

Now, when you talk to a reference, the most important question to ask is, "Does your planner do what she says she's going to do? Does she walk the walk as well as talk the talk?" Ask the reference what he or she wanted the plan to accomplish and then find out if that person followed the plan and if it actually worked. Did the plan cover everything the planner promised it would? It may sound simple, but you'd be surprised how many professionals are out there who don't do what they say they will. For example, I often see other planners at my public presentations. I also see accountants, lawyers, even bankers. Sometimes they're coming to check out what the competition is doing. Sometimes they come to learn what it is that *they* should be doing. Actually, one of my own clients is a guy who works at a bank. He's licensed exactly the way I am, doing a lot of the same stuff, and he's been my client for over twelve years. He came to one of my presentations and decided that he'd rather have me manage his finances than do it himself. And when I asked him about his own job, he said to me, "We don't have the same experience that you have, so we don't do what you do. At the bank, we talk about it, but we don't actually do it." That's exactly what he said to me.

So, talk to the references each planner provides. Ask them tough questions. Go to public seminars. Mingle with their clients if you can. Find out exactly what it is they do, and see if it matches what they *say* they're going to do.

One more point on this. Something that annoys me to no end is how people will try to sell you by saying they're "the best." Everyone does it, regardless of what industry they're in. I deal with people in the aviation industry who do this. For example, salespeople are always telling me they're the best at this or the best at that, and they could be. But I don't want you to tell me you're the best. I want you to *show me*. Because they *should* show me. That's true of aviation companies, plumbers, or financial planners. If the planners you meet keep telling you they're the best, over and over, take it with a grain of salt. If they truly are the best, they shouldn't need to say that. They should trust that the quality of their work is reflected in their reputation.

Where, then, do you go from here? Go meet with three planners. Meet with more if you have to, but make it at least three. Be *very* patient through this process because it's critical that you compare different planners. Find the one who makes you feel comfortable, who speaks your language, who has the best reputation and references. Find someone who will *truly* help you create a plan. If you hit this step hard, you'll have it wrapped up in thirty days or less.

STEP THREE: PUT THE PLAN TOGETHER

Time: thirty days

Here, you and your planner work together to actually create your financial plan. If you've decided what your mission is, if you've written down your goals and values ahead of time, then this stage should go very quickly. It might even be fun! It's a neat experience to see how your plan unfolds. As we discussed in chapter 6, your planner should ask lots of questions and request certain documents from you. You will probably have three or four meetings in person and maybe a couple more over the phone. Then your planner will take all that he or she has learned and will go about researching, writing, and double-checking the plan before presenting it to you.

Once you're holding the plan in your hands, you've arrived at the fourth and final step, the last stage in your journey to change your financial life.

STEP FOUR: IMPLEMENT THE PLAN

Time: thirty days

Technically, this step will last longer than thirty days. After all, you'll be implementing your plan for the rest of your life—and that's a good thing! But it should take only thirty days for you to start noticing changes. Thirty days for you to change your investments, purchase the insurance you need, complete your wills, set up accounts, and correct your taxes if required. Thirty days to start tangibly working towards your goals.

Thirty days for true peace of mind.

Imagine one final scenario. You're driving down the road. As you drive along, you notice the car isn't going as fast as it should. You're moving, but it seems like something is holding you back. No matter. You don't have time to check what's wrong. You have to keep going.

Next you stop to pick up your financial planner. Then you resume driving. Suddenly you notice a horrible burning smell filling the air. You ignore it. Doesn't matter. You've still got your foot on the gas pedal. You're still moving—but slower and slower all the time. At this rate, you'll never reach your destination, and the burning smell is getting worse. Finally, you say, "Something is wrong here."

That's when your planner reaches over and releases the parking brake, which had been on the entire time.

What do you think will happen to you and your car? You'll surge forwards. You'll accelerate. You'll go so fast, you'll think you've gone into warp speed. And, as you do, as you experience that sudden rush of acceleration, the exhilarating feel of speed that you've never felt before nor ever imagined could exist, you'll feel…

Liberated.

That's truly what it's like. You'll feel liberated, like the shackles have come off, like you're finally getting to where you want to go. All of a sudden, your car is going to perform like it never has before. You'll be flying.

And that's all it takes. First, determine your mission. Next, give yourself thirty days to find your planner. Take another thirty days to work with him or her and a final thirty to implement the plan you make together. That's it. It takes only ninety days.

Ninety days to change your financial life. Did you ever think you could do that?

Now, you know you can.

ACKNOWLEDGMENTS

This book could not have been completed without the kind assistance and patience of many people, including my business partner, Warren White, for his time, editing, and encouragement.

To Matt Bailey for helping me put the words to paper and typing and retyping the manuscript.

To my staff and clients for their patience.

And, most importantly, to my wife, Janice, and my son, Justin, for their support and encouragement.

A special thanks to the many professionals in the industry who have added to my experience over the years.

Finally, to my clients, thank you for the trust and respect you have for me as without you I wouldn't have a financial planning practice.

ABOUT THE AUTHOR

Wes Forster is a Certified Financial Planner, Registered Financial Planner, Chartered Financial Planner, and is licensed to sell segregated funds, annuities, GICs, and insurance. Wes has been "planning" things his entire life, but technically, he began his career in the financial services industry in 1984. He started by selling insurance, but it didn't take him long to realize that insurance wasn't going to fix every problem his clients faced. He realized that every aspect of a person's finances is connected and decided to teach his clients how these aspects influence one another.

Soon, Wes understood that the key to changing your financial life was to create a plan. This realization led him to create his own financial planning business, HSI Financial Group Inc. Registered in five provinces, Wes helps people take control of their finances on a daily basis by helping them understand what their values and goals are before creating a plan that will help them reach their intended destinations.

While helping people is perhaps his greatest passion, it's not his only one. Wes loves flying for both business and pleasure, and he is an accomplished pilot. But, most of all, there's nothing he values more than spending time with his family, including his wife, Janice, and his son, Justin.

Wes lives in Kelowna, British Columbia. HSI Financial Group's head office is located in Calgary, Alberta, and can be reached toll-free at 1-888-816-7020. Please visit www.knowyoucan.ca for further information.

Made in the USA
Charleston, SC
19 November 2013